P9-DOC-776

Reflections of
a Peacemaker

Other books by
Mattie J.T. Stepanek

Heartsongs

Journey Through Heartsongs

Hope Through Heartsongs

Celebrate Through Heartsongs

Loving Through Heartsongs

Reflections of
a Peacemaker

A Portrait Through Heartsongs

Mattie J.T. Stepanek

Foreword by Oprah Winfrey

Introduced and Edited by Jennifer Smith Stepanek

**Andrews McMeel
Publishing**

Kansas City

Reflections of a Peacemaker

Copyright © 2005 by Jennifer Smith Stepanek. All rights reserved. Printed in the United States of America. No part of this book may be used or reproduced in any manner whatsoever without written permission except in the case of reprints in the context of reviews. For information, write Andrews McMeel Publishing, an Andrews McMeel Universal company, 4520 Main Street, Kansas City, Missouri 64111.

05 06 07 08 09 RR2 10 9 8 7 6 5 4 3 2 1

ISBN-13: 978-0-7407-5625-2
ISBN-10: 0-7404-5625-7

Library of Congress Control Number: 2005926073

Illustrations by Mattie J.T. Stepanek

Photo courtesy of Randy Sisulak: v

Photos courtesy of Jeni Stepanek: all photos unless otherwise noted

Photos courtesy of Jim Hawkins: 2, 32, 60, 131, 132, 184, 213

Photos courtesy of the International Association of Firefighters: 84, 207

Photo courtesy of the Catholic University of America, Gary Pierpoint: 132

Photo courtesy of Sandy Newcomb: 208

ATTENTION: SCHOOLS AND BUSINESSES

Andrews McMeel books are available at quantity discounts with bulk purchase for educational, business, or sales promotional use. For information, please write to: Special Sales Department, Andrews McMeel Publishing, 4520 Main Street, Kansas City, Missouri 64111.

This book is dedicated to Mattie J.T. Stepanek,
"a poet, a peacemaker, and a philosopher who played."
Thank you for considering, sharing, planting, nurturing, cultivating,
and spreading seeds of hope and peace
for our world, and for the future.

This book is also dedicated to all those in the world who
embrace Mattie's poetry and philosophy of peace and play.
Thank you for considering, sharing, planting, nurturing, cultivating,
and continuing to spread these seeds of hope and peace.
Thank you for your gift to Mattie, and
for our world and the future.

Contents

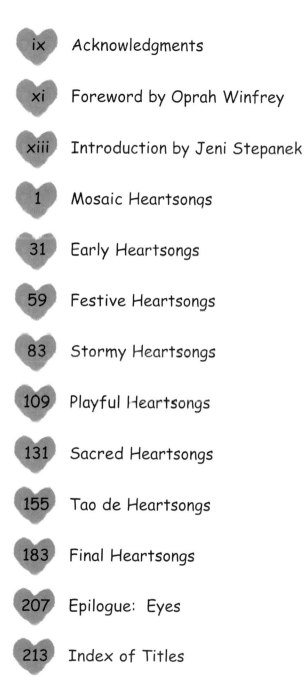

Acknowledgments

My dearest friend, Sandy Newcomb, spent many hours helping me sift through the wealth of materials Mattie left for us. Mattie considered Sandy his "VFABF" (very favorite adult best friend) and her family his "kin." She has truly been our blessing since before Mattie was born, joining us in cheerful celebrations and inspirational endeavors, assisting and supporting us during medical procedures and crises, and sitting with us amid the ashes that have so often been our reality in life.

Diane Tresca, another longtime family friend who shared memories and words from her conversations with Mattie, also had an important role, as I considered changing the title and format of the book. Shelly Heesacker and Bob Balkam, ardent advocates in finding the right publishing home for Mattie's final two manuscripts, have been key architects and engineers in many endeavors to commemorate Mattie's legacy. I am thankful that I was introduced to Jean Lucas, and to Andrews McMeel Publishing, who have been so enthusiastic and caring in preparing and releasing Mattie's final books. And I am thankful to Hyperion/VSP for their role in the publication of Mattie's first five books in the Heartsongs collection.

I will forever be grateful to Bob Ross, Mike Blishak, and other friends at the Muscular Dystrophy Association, and to everyone at Children's National Medical Center in Washington, D.C. (especially the Pediatric Intensive Care Unit and the Volunteer Services), for their gifts of life and hope. And I am grateful to the We Are Family Foundation and Lollipop Theater Network, who together sponsor "Mattie's Movie and Poetry Day" for ill and dying children and their families in hospitals nationwide.

The inspirational organization of this book would not be the same without the generous contributions from so many of Mattie's friends, role models, and heroes, including the foreword by Oprah Winfrey and the chapter tributes offered by Maya Angelou, Jann Carl, Jimmy Carter, Christopher Cross, Chris Cuomo, Fr. Isidore Dixon, Larry King, Jerry Lewis, and Dr. Murray Pollack.

And finally, I thank my son Mattie J.T. Stepanek for sharing his thoughts and insights, his *Reflections of a Peacemaker* that have created this *Portrait Through Heartsongs,* and for allowing me—for allowing each of us—to carry forth his message of hope and peace.

For more information about Mattie or about the MDA Mattie Fund, please visit these Web sites: www.mattieonline.com and www.mdausa.org.

Foreword
by Oprah Winfrey

From the very first moment I met Mattie on my show, which was three years ago, I fell in love with him. We became quick friends, e-mailing each other. I started all of my e-mails to him with "Hello, my guy," and we ended all our e-mails with "I love you and you love me." He was an inspiration and will continue to be an inspiration to me.

It's not often that we find people in our lives who create magic. I found him to be magical. I could not believe so much wisdom, so much power, so much grace, so much strength and love could come from one ten-year-old little boy. . . . I loved his desire to be known for his work and not just to be famous. . . . He e-mailed me on the day that he met Jimmy Carter, saying, "Did you know I met Jimmy Carter today? It was so great because he is famous *and* important. He makes me really think about my life and my purpose here on earth, just like you do. That is good," he said, "because sometimes, especially when things get tough, I have a lot of wondering going on inside my heart and mind. I'm very lucky and blessed to be friends with my heroes. I wish that for other people, too."

We often talked about the sunrises and sunsets, and I shared with Mattie that I wasn't a beach person because there was no need for me to tan. He encouraged me to try the beach anyway, because there were so many other benefits to the beach and sand. He said that he highly recommended this beach that he and his mom visited. He could not understand why everybody wasn't out on the pier at sunrise during their vacation, because he couldn't figure out why people would want to miss a sunrise. . . . I said, "Mattie, most people like to sleep on vacation."

We also talked a lot about dying. He often wrote to me about his feelings about dying, and I shared my feelings about dying with him. He said to me one day, "My body is trying to die more and more each year, even though my spirit is trying to keep it going, even just a little bit longer." He said, "I sometimes get a little depressed or angry when I'm scared about dying. And the boys who live upstairs said that because I got famous, that I should always be happy and never sad. I don't think they understand what it's like to know you have to live your life so fast, because unless I keep getting miracles, my life here won't last. I am happy. I love life. But I also get scared about the pain of dying and about what I will miss because I love living so, so, so much.

"Sometimes I think it would be easier to know for sure when it will happen, but nobody knows for sure. My mom says I float between the possibility of death and the probability of it.

xi

And most times, I am so happy you would never even know I think about it. Maybe it's not depressed I get, but lonely about it because people often don't understand how you can really love life and not be afraid of being dead, but also dread dying and being gone. But I am very lucky and blessed because too many people die and never live their dreams. And some don't even have dreams, or realize them if they do have them. I have big dreams, and I don't stop dreaming them until they happen."

He said to me, "I want to leave so many gifts for people to have when I'm not here anymore. I really do want to be a peacemaker when I die. I want people to remember me someday and say, 'Oh, yes! Mattie! He was a poet, a peacemaker, and a philosopher who played.' I want that in a humble way, not a vain way."

With Mattie, the light of his life shined so brightly that every one of us who knew him, who were honored and had the grace to meet him, will feel the glow for the rest of our lives. I know that his Heartsong has left a heartprint in my life—a heartprint that abides with me even now. I know that many of us believed that when we were with him, talked to him, saw him, that we were witnessing the presence of an angel here on earth. I know for sure that now he has more than earned his wings. Mattie, my guy, I love you and you love me.

Excerpt from Tribute by Oprah Winfrey during the funeral of Mattie J.T. Stepanek on June 28, 2004, Wheaton, Maryland

Introduction

by Jeni Stepanek
(Mattie's mom)

I have a song, deep in my heart,
And only I can hear it . . .
My Heartsong sounds like this—
I love you! I love you!
How happy you can be!
How happy you can make
This whole world be!
And sometimes it's other
Tunes and words, too,
But it always sings the
Same special feeling to me . . .

Excerpt from "Heartsong" by
Mattie J.T. Stepanek, in *Journey Through Heartsongs*
(Hyperion/VSP, 2002)

Mattie J.T. Stepanek loved people and life. Born on July 17, 1990, Mattie was the youngest of four children, each born with a life-threatening neuromuscular disease. The devastating effects of this disease were not realized or diagnosed until all four of the children were born. Mattie never knew his two oldest siblings, Katie and Stevie, who died before he was born. But he was very close to his brother, Jamie, who died when they were both preschoolers. Mattie's earliest creations of poetry during his preschool years developed from his expressions of grief as he coped with the loss of his beloved brother, with the change in his mother's abilities as she developed symptoms and was diagnosed with the adult form of the disease, and with his growing understanding of his own mortality and spirituality due to the disease.

In speeches, Mattie often said, "As I grew, my poetry grew with me. It began with thoughts and words about my brother Jamie and about the concepts of forever and Heaven. But across the years, I have written about senses, about seasons, about nature,

xiii

about journeys, about pain, about laughter, about hope, and a lot about peace. I write about anything that touches the essence of my existence. What I witness, what I feel, what I think, what I fear, what I treasure. In fact, everything that I write comes from some personal experience—the death of a sibling or a friend, a visit to or from Heaven, the excitement of the changing seasons, attitudes and choices that promote peace for individuals and the world . . . I write about life, which is our greatest gift."

Mattie began calling his creations "Heartsongs" when he was about five years old. This was around the same time he told a reporter that his life philosophy was "always remember to play after every storm." Though his poetry grew as he grew, his concept of why Heartsongs matter and his reliance on his life philosophy never changed. On many occasions, Mattie defined a Heartsong as "a person's inner beauty and strength" and "a person's special message and reason to be" in this world. He explained that whatever it is that each person needs and desires most in his or her own heart and life is what that person most needs to offer the world as a gift.

Each person's Heartsong is unique and essential in Mattie's description, even if the message is the same. No two Heartsongs are exactly alike, and no one Heartsong is better than any other one. He has said that it is important to take the time and effort to listen to and share our own Heartsongs, but that it is equally important to take the time and effort to listen to and share the Heartsongs of others, so that we are a world voice, each of us in harmony with every other person around the earth. He also has told us that we should be generous with our own Heartsongs, sharing them with those we encounter who have forgotten or lost the song in their hearts, until their own Heartsongs reawaken and unite to become an integral part of "the festive fabric of life."

Despite the amount of time Mattie spent in the hospital during his last year of life, he worked diligently on many writing and speaking projects related to hope and peace for the world, and for each of us as individuals. He was especially excited about two planned publications. One of these efforts, *Just Peace: A Message of Hope* (Andrews McMeel Publishing, 2006), is a collection of essays, e-mail communications, and other materials in which Mattie examines issues related to personal and world peace, with the support and collaboration of former President Jimmy Carter. The other publication on which Mattie spent a considerable amount of time was this book, his final volume of poetry in his Heartsongs series.

The first five books in the Heartsongs collection contained poems and illustrations created by Mattie from his preschool through preadolescent years organized into themes. Mattie wanted to produce one last book in this format, and he had titled this manuscript *Heartsongs: The Final Collection* many months before he died. He said that he chose the phrase "final collection" for the title not because of the possibility, or even probability, of his early death. Rather, he chose this phrase because he was growing older.

Although he never planned to stop writing or speaking about peace and hope and other matters of importance, Mattie said that any poetry he wrote once he became fourteen years of age would be incorporated into other materials he would create, such as essays, novels, short stories, speeches, philosophy books, and perhaps a biography. But before he made the transition to publishing works as a young adult, Mattie wanted to release one last compilation of poetry that spanned the decade from when he first began expressing his Heartsongs at age three, to his present age at the time, and now for eternity, of thirteen (or "almost fourteen" as Mattie preferred).

Before he died, Mattie asked me if I would continue spreading and nurturing his message of hope and peace for him, including the publication and elucidation of his final two manuscripts. In accepting this mission, I was determined to remain true to Mattie's planned organization and intent. In sifting through all of Mattie's written and recorded materials though, I realized that the collection of poems he had gathered for this book was, in essence, a biographical sketch. Mattie's life, filled with thoughts and reactions, experiences and reflections, became his poetry as he realized and gathered and shaped his reality into words.

Through this book we are given more than a new collection of poetry—we are offered a window into Mattie's life and mind and spirit. In addition, we are offered the reflections of his view through the window from which he looked out into the world, thus the new title for this book, *Reflections of a Peacemaker: A Portrait Through Heartsongs*. I have added an introduction to each chapter that gives readers background information and context for each theme to provide a better understanding of Mattie as a person who faced many life challenges and yet chose to live as "a poet, a peacemaker, and a philosopher who played."

In reading these poems, we enter Mattie's world and gain insight through a child who somehow balanced pain and fear with optimism and faith, and found reason to celebrate Heartsongs and life and to "always remember to play after every storm." And so, in this last volume of Mattie's poetry created across a decade, we are given an extraordinary and final opportunity to witness the uncensored and innocent expressions of a child who lived a lifetime or more in a mere "almost fourteen years." Mattie's poetry inevitably delves into painful issues, such as disability and despair and death of siblings, friends, and self. But it also is rich with imagery and awakens all the senses, as he explores with excited passion the treasured gifts he finds in color, nature, prayer, play, and even in the challenges which sometimes lead to belief in something "bigger and better than the here and now."

His passages are filled with sunrises and sunsets, feathers and seashells, people and peace, pain and hope, faith and frustration, lullabies and laughter, death and dancing, echoes and silhouettes, visions and celebrations, mortality and eternity. Some of it is very simple and sweet, and some of it is profound and even dark. But all of it is necessary, essential, to this collection that paints a portrait of wisdom and understanding from one child, one person, who offers a message of hope and peace for the world. This book is the reality experienced and expressed by a child who, to the very end of his breath, loved people and life.

The entries in this book were chosen from the thousands of poems, essays, journal entries, and letters Mattie left behind. It is organized into eight thematic or age-related chapters of poetry that collectively create a tapestry of life from its darkest challenges to its brightest celebrations. One essay has also been included as an epilogue. The essay is actually a chapter from an unfinished novel Mattie began writing just a few months before his final hospitalization. When I read the passage for the first time after his death, it seemed to me to illustrate a reflection of how Mattie would create his own Heaven, if he were a part of the design. It is clear that Mattie loved people and life so much that his Heaven would be earth all over again, even with the pain and challenges that are folded into the joy and blessings of each day.

On March 7, 2004, Mattie penned his last poem, and called it "Final Thoughts." The following day, he went into heart failure. He died three and a half months later, on June 22. One of the last statements Mattie made during the weeks before his death was that he was "a man of many thoughts, and a man of many, many words." He also asked if he had "done enough" in his life to plant and nurture seeds of hope and peace for children, for adults, for nature, and for the future. As his mother, I reassured him that he had done everything he came to earth to do . . . he was truly the best person he could be. And, as a member of the human race and a citizen of this earth, I am blessed with reassurance that Mattie J.T. Stepanek was truly the "ambassador of humanity" he aspired to be.

Mosaic Heartsongs

In so many ways, we are the same.
Our differences are unique treasures.
We have, we are, a mosaic of gifts
To nurture, to offer, to accept . . .

Excerpt from "For Our World" by Mattie J.T. Stepanek,
in *Hope Through Heartsongs* (Hyperion/VSP, 2002)

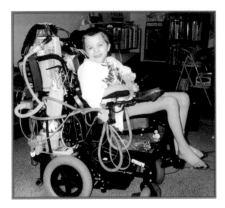

PREVIOUS PAGE: Mattie with his original homemade Heartsongs collections, spring 1998

TOP: Mattie fishing off the pier in Nags Head, North Carolina, summer 1999

BOTTOM LEFT: Mattie, "I am the walrus, goo goo g'joob," summer 2002

BOTTOM RIGHT: Mattie just home from a six-month stay in the Pediatric ICU, summer 2001

A very young poet once wrote, "The poet does not see the writing on the wall. He sees the wall, that's all. But for many others goes his clarion call, for they do not see the wall." I think that must have been written for Mattie Stepanek because he does see the wall. And he may not know everything, but he knows so much about life to be so young and so wise, to know that the heart makes the rules about living well and that does not mean living without pain. It does certainly. . . . It does not mean being at the top of one's form all the time. It means being in love, loving, daring to love, risking love, risking making oneself courteous and kind . . . that really is high intelligence. I like Mattie a lot. I'd even go far enough to say I love Mattie. As a poet, I look at him as another poet. And as a human being, I look at him as a wonderful, huge, old, wise, kind, intelligent, rich human being . . . though he's not yet in his teens, but that has nothing to do with the Heartsong. I'm proud that he has enough courage to stand up, inside himself, and be a representative of all human beings.

I think Mattie Stepanek is about as good as we get. My name is Maya Angelou and I wrote a poem called "And Still I Rise," and I think I may have written it also for Mattie Stepanek—"You may write me down in history with your bitter twisted lies. You may trod me in the very dirt, but still, like dust, I'll rise." That is for Mattie Stepanek and all those who love him. For the people—his mother, his family and friends, beloveds, for all the readers, for all those who are lonely and lost and disinherited and disenchanted and dispossessed, Mattie Stepanek knows a lot about that. So I think he is about as good as we get.[1]

[He] was a thirteen-year-old white boy, poet, American. I am a seventy-six-year-old woman, poet, African American. We liked each other. We, in fact, held hands. I loved his love for the human spirit. He believed that the human spirit could overcome wars, and rumors of wars, hate, destruction, cruelty, brutality. He thought that love cures things. I do, too, so we had no difficulty coming together and holding hands. One thing I know is that spirit never dies. I am grateful to Mattie Stepanek for coming here, for being here, for being present while he was here. And I'm grateful that his spirit remains with us. I am grateful I know this is a better world because of Mattie Stepanek.[2]

—Dr. Maya Angelou
(Poet, Humanitarian, and Reynolds Professor of
American Studies, Wake Forest University, North Carolina)

From Tributes to Mattie by Maya Angelou
1. Second Annual Heartsongs Gala to benefit the Muscular Dystrophy Association, February 2004.
2. MDA Labor Day Telethon, September 2004.

3

Mosaic Heartsongs

Mattie believed that every person ever created had some purpose, some reason to be in this world, whether that person existed for a mortal second or for more than a century. He also believed that many people could offer similar gifts, rooted in the same purpose or reason for being, and yet each person's contribution and existence was truly irreplaceable and essential. Differences, he said, are unique treasures, and he could never understand why we choose to argue about things that make life worthy and interesting to witness, to explore, and to appreciate. It is easy to see then, why the concept of the world as "a mosaic of gifts" is an ongoing theme in Mattie's poetry.

The mosaic of life as Mattie considered it was both simple and complex. Mattie viewed all of humanity and creation as one great mosaic, but he also saw each individual person as a unique mosaic within the collective tapestry of the world gift—trillions of individual mosaics, past and present and future, within the one great mosaic of life. In his perspective, we can have a sense of the big picture without scrutinizing every aspect, but the tapestry, the mosaic, is never truly complete without the inclusion, the consideration, of every single piece of the portrait.

In this book, we are offered a mosaic of Mattie's thoughts and words and passages—his gifts for our world. This first chapter, Mosaic Heartsongs, gives a sampling of many aspects of Mattie's writing and of his life. He writes about poetry, playing with words, simile and metaphor, free verse and rhyme, natural rhythm and forced meter. There are lessons of pleasure and of urgency, deliberations on mortality and on spirituality, and responses to nature and to violence. And, there are insights about truth and love and hope, and about things that matter, or should matter, to people and to the world. Inevitably, there will be people who feel drawn to his lighter poems, and there will be people who feel drawn to his deeper, complex poems. But in this mosaic, all elements are essential as they come together to create the true reflection and portrait of a young poet, peacemaker, and philosopher who played.

Duties as Designed

The job of the poet
Is to give birth to the words
That give breath to expressions
Of the essence of life.
The job of the poet
Is to leave stains of the storms
Yet echo laughter of the light
That is seen from the soul.
The job of the poet
Is to weave ashes of yesterthoughts
Into silhouettes that rise gently
On the horizon of dawning hope.
The job of the poet
Is to create and to capture
And to spirit and to script
The pulse of life.

February 14, 2003

Doctor Lesson

I will not be the reason
Maya buys a ticket and
Boards the train to Bangkok.
I will not be the reason
She holds her head with purpose
While her shoulders droop
For the wasting of minds.
I will not be the reason
She pens a lesson on looking
Life in the eye with the heart
Of one who has risen
From amid the ashes of
Things without roots or right.
No, I will reason
And I will resolve
And recite with a humble pride
That sings the song of my soul
To the world as it is
So that perhaps,
It can soar to heavenly heights
And be the reason
It was meant to be.

May 23, 2002

Morning Crunch

The cold melon skies of morning
Slowly streak through milky clouds
As the orange juice sun rises
Behind coffee and burnt toast branches.
I would like to stop and share
Magic-star cereal with
The few winter birds,
But the hands on the clock
Keep pointing to the day saying,
"Hurry up, or you'll miss the bus!"

February 9, 1998

Filling the Space

Bridge-clouds are Angel-ladders
That space between Heaven and Earth.
The Angels and God
Come to us in such special ways.
And when they disappear,
And we do not see the bridge-clouds,
We do not need to worry or wonder,
Because we know that They are here.
The clouds are just reminders
That they come, and
That they stay, and
That they are really always
In Heaven and on earth and
All that space between them.

July 28, 1996

Sunrise

The last two stars of the night,
The moon dimming into day,
Pink fingers of light reaching
Into less gray skies,
Dolphins playing school
In new morning waves,
Golden cloud-streaks greeting
The dawning ball of fire,
Up from the ocean . . .
Sunrise on the pier.

July 16, 1998

Absolutely

One of my most
Favorite colors is ruby—
A bright pinkish-red.
And, if you add
A twinch of orange,
It would make a
Beautiful desert sunset
Over Cowboy Land.
And that is my absolute
Most favorite color.

July 6, 1998

6:00 a.m. Revelation

Today is July 1.
I've already finished
Eating breakfast,
And Mommy didn't
Change the calendar
Off of June yet!
How's my birthday
Ever going to get here?

> July 1, 1994
> (6:00 a.m.)

Legacy

Tomorrow,
I will turn into four years old.
But one day,
I will turn into
Twenty-five years old.
If I was twenty-five,
I could put three gumballs
Into my mouth
At the same time.
I could read big,
Mommy books,
And even the
Bible book by myself.
I could hang upside-
Down in a tree.
And I could have children
Of my very own.
And when I had children,
I would name them
Special children's names,
Like Brown and Blaine,
And Tessie and Tad,
And Patch and Hope.
But the first one would be
Jamie.

> July 16, 1994

9

The Gift of a Name

My name is
Mattie Joseph Thaddeus Stepanek.
My name fits my personality
Like my skin fits my body.
Mattie is from Matthew,
Which means "Gift of God."
I wasn't supposed to live,
Yet, here I am a decade old.
Joseph is a good strong family name,
And represents a
Happy and peaceful death.
Thaddeus is my Confirmation name,
And it means "loving and friendly."
I took the name because
St. Jude Thaddeus is the
Patron saint of hopeless situations,
Like my life, and because
I can share it with my brother Jamie,
Whose Confirmation name is Jude.
Although my last name, Stepanek,
Doesn't well-represent my
Irish and Scottish ancestry,
It is unique and so it is perfect
To top off my other names.
My name is
Mattie Joseph Thaddeus Stepanek.
I am a gift of God,
I am a strong family person,
I am loving and friendly,
I am unique in life, and
I am proud to have
My special name.

April 15, 2000

On Growing Up (Part VI)

So many thoughts on growing up.
So many things to do and be.
When I was little, I wanted to be a doctor
Healing children and people.
But children and people die,
Even when doctors do their best job.
And even though it's okay, it's still sad,
And I don't want to be a doctor anymore.
Now I am older and I want to be other things.
I want to be a writer, and teach people about living.
I want to be a daddy, and love my children forever.
I want to be a Grandmaster in Martial Arts, and
Help everyone learn the way to combine
Their bodies and their minds with their spirits.
And when I am a writer, a daddy, and a Grandmaster,
I will be a peacemaker, and remind everyone
In the whole wide world about their Heartsongs.
The world is such a wonderful place, and
Each life is such a wonderful gift, and
Our Heartsongs are so wonderful inside us . . .
But people forget this, unless a peacemaker is there.
So many thoughts about growing up,
And so many things to do and be.
And then I remember why I don't want to be a doctor,
And that no one ever knows
If they will grow up, or not.
So really, the most important
Goal of all in growing up,
Is that I want to BE.

July 17, 1997

Best of the Best

My favorite colors are
Pink and orange.
Sometimes,
I say they are "sunset."
God's favorite color is "world."
My favorite number is "five,"
And also twenty-five,
Forty-five, and other
Numbers that end in five.
God's favorite number is "all,"
From "nothing to for-everything."
My favorite hand is my "left,"
And my left eye, ear, and foot.
God's favorite is "everyone's"
Hands, eyes, ears, and feet.
My favorite language is
"Sweet voices" like in lullabies,
That sing to us in English, or
Korean, or Sign Language.
God's knows all languages,
But His favorite is the
"Language of children."
My favorite flavor is "chocolate."
God's favorite flavor is "rainbow."
My favorite places are the
"North Pole, Hawaii,
Australia, Ireland, and Heaven."
God's favorite is "every place,"
Except for Hell, because Hell is the
Baddest place where devils live.

My favorite things to do are to
"Pray to God, read books, write
Poems and stories, watch movies,
And play with Mommy
And with friends and with Legos."
God's favorite things to do are to
"Say 'good job, people!' and
Put His hand on my shoulder
When I behave and be like Him."
My favorite song is the "Heaven
Is a Wonderful Place" song.
God's favorite song is
"Glory to God in the Highest."
My favorite things in the world are
"God, Mommy, and Mr. Bunny."
God's favorite things are
"His people."
My favorite dream-wish is
"Teaching peace, and also getting
My Black Belt and being in Heaven
With my brothers and sister."
God's favorite dream-wish is about
"Goodness and kindness and the
End of hating, fighting, and war."
Wow!
That's a lot of neat favorites!
But God wins.
God wins the "Best of the Best."
And I wish I could give Him
The "Gift of Peace" as first prize.

April 16, 1996

Pleasant Dreams (I)

Last night I had a
Very happy dream.
I dreamed that I sent
A red-heart balloon
Up to Heaven for Jamie.
And when it got
Stuck in a tree,
Jamie came and
Got it out of the tree,
And took it
Up to Heaven so
He could play with it.
He was smiling,
And smiling,
And smiling.
He made it go
Around and around,
And up and down.
And I was smiling,
And Jamie was smiling,
And all of Heaven
Was smiling, too.

October 17, 1993

About Wealth

The richest
Person is the one
Who is
Friends
With all
The earth.

November 29, 2000

Grasp of Truth

If you have
Enough breath
To complain
About anything,
You have more than
Enough reason
To give thanks
About something.

May 6, 2001

13

About Living (Part III)

I wanted to live
To be
One hundred and one
Years old.
But that is no
Longer my goal.
When I die,
I die.
I cannot predict.
I cannot control.
I cannot change
What is to be,
Which is what it is
And will be
What it will be.
I wanted to live
To be,
And not die.
But,
While I'm alive,

I live
To the fullest.
I treasure each sunrise.
I remember each sunset.
I dance every dance and
I sing every song and
I celebrate every moment.
I wanted to live
To be.
And,
I am spending my time
On earth before death
Living,
Rather than dying,
And not wasting a moment
Of the precious gifts
Of time and
Of life and
Of being, for now.

July 23, 2003

14

Mosaic Heartsongs

My Special Family: My Kin

My family is very special to me,
And, my family is very unique.
I have my mommy, whom I dearly love.
My two brothers and my sister are dead.
So, I have kin.
Kin are people who love each other,
And feel very close to each other.
They are not blood related.
But, that is very much okay.
Kin do things together, and
They take care of each other,
As well as their possessions.
Among my kin are people
Who are like fathers to me.
There are also people
Who are like brothers, sisters,
Grandfathers, grandmothers,
And other mothers to me.
I love them all dearly, just like family.
And, they all love me
And love my mommy dearly,
Just like family.
And, just like family,
They help Mommy and me
Live our lives peacefully.
And, we help them in return,
Just like family.
My family is made of
My mommy and me,
And many kin members.
My family is unique, and
I love my family very much.

April 17, 2000

About My Mommy

To me, my mommy is very special.
I love her and trust her with all of my heart.
She saved me when I was a baby.
She gave me life not only in birth,
But in bringing me back to life on earth
When God welcomed me in Heaven a little too early.
Then, she taught me . . .
How to be peaceful and live in harmony.
How to be kind and generous,
And to think of others before myself.
How to think and start out positive,
And to mediate, because fighting
Is no way to figure things out.
She has been teaching me life lessons
For as long as I can remember.
And every one has a major part
In my past, my present, and my future life.
Throughout our life,
We have lived through many things together.
Bad times and good, sad times and happiness,
Danger and safety, violence and peace,
Anger and love, and hatred and harmony.
I know that no matter what,
We will always be together.
The Dynamic Duo, forever.
Each day we face a new step in the future,
Inseparable and fun-seeking, together.
I love you, Mommy,
And we will always be Together Forever.
Together.
Forever.

December 16, 1999

16

Friends Helping Friends

The spirit of Will
Is with me this week,
I'll toast to my friend,
About him I'll speak.
The spirit of Will
Is deep in my heart,
Although he's not here,
Of camp, he's a part.
The spirit of Will
Is in need of some hope,
He's hurting a lot,
He's trying to cope.
The spirit of Will
Can be strengthened by us,
Let's all let him know
That his spirit's a must.
Let the spirit of Will
Be with us this week,
Let's toast to our friend,
Let him know he's unique.
Let the spirit of Will
Be deep in each heart,
For the distance of space
Cannot keep us apart.

          June 17, 2000

The Katie Poem

Katie is . . .
A joyful person.
A spreader of cheer.
A bringer of hope.
A lover of life,
And people.
Katie has . . .
An open heart.
A spirit for each cause.
A generous angel soul,
On earth.
Katie offers . . .
A trust for the future.
A thought from the past.
A celebration of the present,
Our gift.
For all that Katie offers,
For all that Katie has,
For all that Katie is . . .
We thank You, God.

          September 1, 2000

For Lauren

I love you.
I love you very much.
You will always be my
Beautiful child-bride,
Even if you are moving to
The other side of the country.
You are like a shining sun.
I will wait for you.
I will wait for you
To come back, in a year,
Or four years, or maybe more.
I will wait for you
And we will really get married
When we are grown up.
I will find a shiny pebble for you,
And save it so that you will
Know how much I love you.
It will be sunset peach
And pink and orange,
And it will be so smooth,
And strong.
It is very sad thinking about
You leaving,
But I really, really love you.
And I will wait for you
And give you
Our shiny pebble
When you come home.

July 20, 1997

Thought

Love is
Peaceful.
It is an
Anytime
Gift.

February 13, 1998

Homily Lesson

Give a gift of a smile,
Give a gift of a hug,
Give a gift of a
Helping hand . . .
And you give a gift
From the heart
That is priceless.

December 7, 1998

Key to America

From the beginning,
To now,
Through future,
There are keys to life.
Our country,
Was, is, and will be
Built on the
Faiths and beliefs
And struggles of people,
For people,
In the name of freedom.
A key in success
Was recognizing
The symbols of our country.
A key in our hearts
Is creating
A land of the free and
A home for the brave.
A key, still waiting,
Will unlock
Our peace with the world,
To share throughout.
When we have all three,
We shall fully honor the
Patriotic words that are Key.

January 27, 2001

Could Be

Things aren't like they could be.
Times could be more peaceful—
A murdering could be a reason for
People to be shocked and sad.
Dropping a bomb could be a reason for
People to be stunned and afraid.
Disrespecting could be a reason for
People to be distressed and embarrassed.
Times could be more prayerful—
Halloween could be active fun,
But also a Holy Night.
Christmas could be represented in a store,
But also truly a Holy Day.
Easter could be sweet with candy.
But also more fully a Holy Season.
Things aren't like they could be.
But the times seem so popular,
Even without being so
Peaceful and prayerful as they could be.
So these things, as they are,
Not as they were in the beginning,
Might not ever end.
And so,
I am shocked, and I am sad, and
I am afraid, and I am embarrassed.
I wish things were more peaceful, and
I wish things were more prayerful, so
We were more like a Holy People,
In all things and in all times—
Like it could be.

September 26, 1998

19

Note to Bosnia

I need to send a note to Bosnia,
To help the people understand
About peace and about war,
And especially about Heartsongs.
I need to tell them about
Saving the earth and the people
And the life, now and after we die.
This is what my note will say:

Dear Bosnia,
I have heard about you having wars,
And I really want it to stop,
Because we can spread peace and
Heartsongs around the world,
Instead of anger and hating.
If we just stop the fighting and killing
And start some hugging and kissing,
We could all say "I am sorry" together,
And there would be no need for wars.
I am sending you some poems I wrote
To help you remember about peace
In our world, and about the children.
Children stop their arguments quickly,
And then they go on loving and playing.
Children need grown-ups though,
To help them grow up.
Children do what the grown-ups say,
So please do what the children need,
And stop the wars and fighting.
We must lay down our weapons
And become Family again.
Everyone has gotten too interested
In the power of hate, but instead,
We should be interested in the power of love.

20

In families, when there is hate,
There is pain and separation.
In countries, when there is hate,
There is war and separation,
And the people die . . .
The grown-ups, and the children.
I am a child, and I have a Heartsong,
And I am trying to help you have one, too,
By sharing mine with you.
I want to grow up.
I want to have peace.
If you get interested in the good,
Please send me a letter.
If you stay interested in the bad,
Please still send me a letter,
Because I will pray and write again,
And at least we will be talking about it.
And then, maybe other countries with war
Will want us to write to them, too.
I love you, and all people of the earth.
                In peace, Mattie Stepanek

I will mail this letter to Bosnia, and know
That God was in my heart when I wrote it.
Maybe, one of the people or one of the soldiers
Will read it aloud to the country of people,
And maybe, someone will hear the note
And feel the words and
Remember their Heartsong . . .
And that can be the beginning of peace,
And the beginning of the ending of war.

          October 21, 1996

Vultures Play

The vultures like it
In the mountains.
Why?
So they can play in
The wind tides.
When the wind tide is
Strong and heavy,
The vultures go straight
Up and let the wind
Carry them above the
Tips of the trees.
When the wind tide is
Weak and soft,
The vultures go straight
Up and peacefully, calmly,
Soar above the
Tips of the trees . . .
Always watching.

August 11, 1998

For Sir Blake

Brave, strong, and serious
Pattern, so fiery and furious,
An animal,
Loved by mankind,
Such a beauty is hard to find.
Swiftly moving, a gift to see,
Your pattern is a mystery,
A clash of colors,
Bright and black
Hidden in nature,
Ready to attack.
We love a tiger's bravery,
Though its true pattern,
We cannot see.
Your immortal might,
Impervious
To our mortal sight,
Yet curious.

December 23, 2002

Self-Report Card

Sometimes,
I think God made a mistake.
Sometimes,
I think I should not be here
All alive on earth.
Sometimes,
I think maybe Jamie,
Or Katie or Stevie should
Have lived on earth, and Mattie
Should have died into Heaven.
Sometimes,
I think that even though
I am smart and thoughtful,
That I am not really a good person.
No matter what I try to do,
I fail.
It doesn't matter that you can
Read or write or think or be
When you don't do it right, or·
When you do it too much, or·
When you do it too little, or
When you talk or move too much
While you are doing it all.
Sometimes,
I really, really think
God made a mistake,
And the wrong kid lived.

February 8, 1996

The Singing of Crickets

Shhhh . . .
Listen carefully, and
You can hear the crickets singing.
If you listen with your ears,
You can hear cheerful chirping.
But if you listen with your heart,
You will hear voices singing.
They are singing:

> *I love you very much,*
> *Oh world!*
> *I love you very much,*
> *Oh Heavens and Earth!*
> *I love you very much,*
> *Oh nature and people!*
> *I love you very much,*
> *Oh everything, everywhere,*
> *Everyone in the world!*

Shhhh . . .
Listen to the crickets with your ears.
Then close your eyes, and
Listen to the crickets with your heart,
And hear and feel a song of peace!

August 23, 1996

23

Mosaic Heartsongs

Simile Lesson

Sometimes,
I am as angry
As a bull seeing red,
And I sound like a
Dog who is barking when
A cat has stolen its house.
My voice is
Like an angry typhoon,
And my eyes flash
Like a lighting match.
I am a child who is
As restless as
A swarm of hornets,
And my heart feels
Like I am trying to
Beat Jesse Owens in a race.
But then,
I realize that my spirit feels
Like dark clouds
When they look
Like stale black ice cream,

And my mind is
Like fog on a Viking morning.
And I know that
My words must never sound
Like I am speaking
Between the lines,
Because the river of life
Runs as deep as
The Words of Jesus Christ.
And then,
My soul becomes
As bright as
The new day's first
Beam peeking over the ocean,
And my smile becomes
Like a radiant rainbow,
Because I can once again
See the Son shine
Brilliantly looking
Like the ruby eye of a tiger.

March 31, 2000

My Heaven-Wish

When I go to Heaven,
The first thing I will do
Is see the face of God,
And give Him a big hug.
Next, I will see
My brothers and sister
Who are waiting for me
And watching over me.
Then, I will ask God
For two things—
To meet the saints and
Famous but dead
Peacemakers, and
To give me
My Angel wings.
In Heaven, I will live
With my earthly family—
My mom and
My brothers and sister,
And celebrate
In my fantasy space—
With characters
From favorite books.
I will live without
Extra oxygen.
I will never
Be hurt or sick or tired.

I will never have
Apnea or bradycardia.
I will never need
A wheelchair or ventilator.
I will explore otherly-worlds.
I will paint the rainbows.
I will help out
Everywhere in Heaven.
And my forever-age will be
Ten-and-one-half earth years.
But my biggest Heaven-wish
Will be to continue
Writing books and poems.
I will visit the spirits
Considering their Heaven
To cheer them up and
To inspire them
Toward their eternal goal, so
That their vision of a perfect
Forever can become a reality.
In doing this,
I will continue
My earth-wish—
I will forever
Be a peacemaker,
And share my
Heartsongs with others.

May 2, 2000

Pleasant Dreams (II)

One night,
My brother, Jamie,
Will come back to me.
And he will sleep in his bed,
And I will sleep in his bed,
Which is my bed now.
We will be sleeping
Together, in our bed.
And Jamie will smile.
And Mattie will smile.
And we will be smiling together.
And the flower-cemetery
And Heaven
Will miss Jamie,
But Mattie will not,
Because, he will be with me.
One night,
This will really happen.
I know it will.

Jamie did not say it to me,
But I still know it.
It will happen in a few days
After Halloween,
Because Jamie is happy
In Heaven,
And he wants me to be happy
In my new house, too.
And Heaven will still be
A wonderful place,
Because Jamie will go back there
After he comes to sleep with me.
But that night,
Jamie's and my bed will be
A wonderful place, too,
Because we will be
Together again.
I will not see Jamie,
And I will not hear Jamie,
And I will not touch Jamie . . .
But I will feel Jamie,
And I will know he is there,
One night.

October 29, 1993

A Snowman in Heaven

One time,
I built a snowman.
But then,
The snowman melted.
I was not sad, though.
When the snowman melted,
It died.
It did not have
Muscles-and-bones anymore.
They were gone into the ground.
But what made the snowman
Happy and special
Was called the spirit.
And the snowman spirit
Went up into Heaven.
Now Jamie has
A snowman in Heaven.
He is so happy.
And Katie and Stevie are happy.
And Danny is happy.
And all the children who died
And live in Heaven are happy.
I shared my snowman with them.
And when it snows again,
I will make another snowman.
And when it dies,
They will have another
Snowman in Heaven.

January 17, 1994

Color Choice

My favorite color
Has always been sunset—
Pink and orange swirled
With purple, gray, and brown.
I have a second favorite color—
Rainbow.
A rainbow has all of my
Favorite sunset colors,
And also all the colors
That are in the sunrise
And in all the fish and birds
And in all the people
That God made.
Some of the kids at my school
Say that pink and orange
Are girls' colors.
But I don't think so
Because boys like
Sunsets too.
And I know that rainbows
Are for boys and girls,
Because they have
Pink and orange and brown
And grey and purple and blue.
I don't think girls and boys
Should have their own colors.
I think God wants us
To share colors,
And to like them all
Because they are all
A gift to us.

January 31, 1995

27

Earth Jewels

Thank You, God,
For the jewels of the earth.
For emerald—
Grass and leaves
Glittering after the rain.
For silver—
Gray of branches
Glimmering in the sun.
For onyx—
Wisdom of leopard spots
Growing inside tree bark.
For ruby—
Red leaves in starlight
Sparkling like sprinkles.
For sapphire—
Greatness of clear skies
Touching Heaven to earth.
For gold—
Beauty of wood and sap
Sustaining new tree sticks.
Thank You, God,
For these
And so many other
Colors of the earth,
Jewels seen with the heart.

July 23, 1997

Marigold Evening

As I sit outside
Reading my book,
I see a golden tree.
Fading leaves of brown
And yellow, announce the
Season's coming.
As I witness the fall-time
Fading the tree,
I see a buttercup sky
Disappearing above me.
The slowly setting sun,
A towheaded evening ball,
It whispers the same as
The golden tree, the
Season's colorful presence.
As I observe the leaves
Swirling in descent,
And I lose the glow
Fading with the sun,
Nature's day-song blooms to night.
Together, they announce
The setting of the season.

October 4, 2001

Night Light

The sky glows
Cherub night light,
An ebullient blue
Of the gentlest ocean.
The sky tires
Into darkness,
Seraphim kisses
Twinkling stars
Into guards for
Never-resting earth folk.
The sky grows
Shadows, rising
With the passing of time,
The heavens even'ing
Into a silhouette
Of times now transpired.
The sky sighs,
Ebbing with tides
Of pre-dawn nothingness,

And yet,
Seas of everything created,
Tucked into waves
Of leftover memories,
Angelic rocking and
Dreams, wishes now expired.
The sun rises
Caressing spirits
With the passing of time
And the promise of hope
And the belief of life
That gets better with age
As we edge into
The day that once was
Our distant tomorrow.
The sun glows and tires
And grows and sighs
In the truth of our days
Illuminating our nights
By the great I Am,
Our past,
Our present,
Our future,
Our light in time.

March 8, 2002

29

Tonight's Prayer

Dear God,
Thank You for brothers, and
Thank You for sisters, and
Thank You for friends when
Brothers and sisters die. And
Thank You for feathers, and
Thank You for seashells, and
Thank You for babies that
Come from mommies' love.
Thank You, God,
For all these things.
Amen.

August 13, 1994

Early Heartsongs

And do you know what is the most
Special window of all?
The window in your heart,
That's between the Heaven-in-the-earth,
And the Heaven-in-the-sky.

Excerpt from "The Importance of Windows"
by Mattie J.T. Stepanek, in *Heartsongs* (Hyperion/VSP, 2002)

PREVIOUS PAGE: Mattie going for a drive, summer 1994

TOP LEFT: Mattie with his brother, Jamie, Halloween 1992

TOP RIGHT: Mattie enjoying a summer afternoon, 1995

BOTTOM: Mattie "hooked up" to all of his nighttime equipment, fall 1993

Tonight, an hour that could well change your life. It changed mine. At a time when the world is at war, this boy makes more sense than a lot of world leaders. . . . His real name is Matthew Joseph Thaddeus Stepanek. We like to call him Mattie. . . .[1] He started writing poetry when he was three years old. A truly amazing kid . . . battling an incurable disease, celebrating life every single day. A best-selling poet. A would-be peacemaker . . . inspiring millions with a message of hope. . . .[2] He'll break your heart and he'll make it soar at the same time. Mattie J.T. Stepanek has become an American legend.[3]

Every once in a while, life introduces you to somebody who helps put everything else into perspective. Someone who makes you realize that your problems are not such a big deal. Someone who makes you want to count your blessings and try to do your best every minute of every day. Mattie J.T. Stepanek was one of those rare somebodies. Mattie was an incredible kid, gifted and gutsy, and a very good friend to this program. I first sat down with him in April of 2002. The show was a gift. . . . Mattie accomplished a lot in his very short life. Despite the pain he endured, he always turned toward the light. The smile, his attitude, and his spirit made you feel so much better about life, just being in the same room with him. Mattie, thank you so much for being such an inspiration. You left us much too soon, pal, and we're going to miss you.[4]

—Larry King

(Host of CNN's *Larry King Live*)

Excerpts from *Larry King Live* shows featuring Mattie J.T. Stepanek
1. April 2002.
2. September 2002.
3. February 2003.
4. June 2004.

Early Heartsongs

E xploring the environment and make-believe, learning new words and ideas, developing self-help and motor skills, understanding relationships and friendships . . . these are some of the many activities enjoyed by typical preschool-aged children. In many ways, Mattie's earliest years were no different than those of other youngsters. He was curiously enchanted by books and stories and movies filled with vivid imagery and characters that fed his growing imagination. He was eager to practice new language concepts and muscle coordination during play and art projects. And he was delightfully enthusiastic about social interactions and opportunities for conversation with other children and adults.

In other ways, however, Mattie's preschool years and development were unique and vastly different from the norm. By the time Mattie was three years old, he had experienced the death of his best friend and brother, Jamie. Mattie knew he and Jamie were born with the same neuromuscular disease. Mattie also was aware of the brief lives of his two other siblings, Katie and Stevie. Both of them died before Mattie was born, yet he felt a strong connection to them. Additionally, between the ages of three and four, Mattie began to experience a decline in his own health, another child with whom he was friends died, and he watched his mother go from riding him on the back of her bicycle to more and more limited physical abilities, and eventually complete reliance on a power wheelchair for mobility.

During a developmental period when most children are learning to simply label feelings of happiness and sadness, excitement and anger, Mattie was learning to cope with the intense emotions of traumatic loss and grief, and to process the frustration that comes with the growing realization of personal limitations and challenges. As he struggled to make sense of the realities of his life, Mattie became aware of issues of mortality and spirituality, peril and resilience, fear and empathy. Extraordinarily talented with verbal skills, and gifted with wisdom and understanding even beyond his advanced knowledge and academic skills, Mattie found hope and peace through creativity, imagination, and capturing written expressions of his experiences and reflections on life.

This chapter, Early Heartsongs, offers a chronological collection of passages from Mattie's first year of creating poetry—June 22, 1993, to June 22, 1994. These dates were chosen to offer readers a comparative framework with Mattie's final chapter and year of life spanning from June 22, 2003, to June 22, 2004. Though there are many entries filled with the delightfully humorous observations of a preschool child, much of his earliest poetry deals with the unavoidable issues of disability and death, and the developmental use of familiar and concrete characters to cope with uncomfortable and abstract situations and sentiments.

34

Early Heartsongs

When I Grow Up . . .

When I get a little-bit-bigger,
I will be Jamie-D.
She is my friend.
Then I will play soccer,
And be rich and sweaty,
Like my friend, Jamie-D.

When I get even-bigger,
I will be Ms. Michele.
She is my teacher.
Then I will hug all the little children,
And play with them and listen to them,
Like my teacher, and my friend, Ms. Michele.

When I get very-big,
I will be Dr. Terry Flotte.
He is my doctor.
Then I will help people and give them check-ups.
I will listen with a stethoscope and look in their ears,
And go to their house before they die.
Just like Dr. Terry Flotte did before my brother died.
I will help people feel better and be happy,
Like my doctor, and my friend, Dr. Terry Flotte.

When I grow up, and turn into
Jamie-D., Ms. Michele, and Dr. Terry Flotte,
I will turn them all back into Mattie.
Then I will be a soccer player, a teacher, a doctor,
And everybody's friend . . .
And I will be me.
The end.

Summer 1993

35

Griefwork

Today I miss Jamie.
I am sad.
Last week
I threw a penny
Into the wishing fountain
At the stores.
I wished and I wished
That I held
Jamie's hand tighter,
And Mommy, too,
So maybe,
He wouldn't really die.

                    June 22, 1993

Refrigerator Art

I drew a picture for Jamie.
It's a smiley-face . . .
But this one has a sad-smile.
It's a sad-face.
I drew a rainbow for Jamie.
It's a brown rainbow . . .
And gray.
Jamie is happy in Heaven.
But sometimes . . .
I miss him.

                    August 4, 1993

Cherubic Pleas

Today . . . I am sad.
Today . . . I cry.
Today . . . I am angry.
Today . . . I stomp my foot.
I want Jamie to come back . . .
Today.
I miss him.
Today . . .
I'm just a little black rain cloud.

                    September 6, 1993

In Heaven

Happy birthday to you,
Happy birthday to you,
Happy birthday dear Stevie,
Happy birthday to you . . .
In Heaven.
I asked Mommy if
I could come to Heaven,
And have cake
And ice cream with you . . .
But Heaven is Forever,
And I am not Forever, yet.
I want to give you a BIG hug.
A big birthday hug and kiss,
In Heaven.
I want to help you unwrap
Where the
Wild Things Are presents,
And *Pinocchio*.
But, I can't.
So we will get you a balloon,
And you can watch it
In Heaven.
I will make it go
Around and around,
And up and down . . .

Then you will
Laugh and smile.
And I will play
Peek-a-boo with you,
So the baby in
Your picture here can laugh,
Even though
You are six years old
In Heaven.
And I will eat cake
And ice cream,
And sing to you,
About fishing and
Lollipops and bumblebees . . .
And you will be So happy.
And Katie and Jamie
Can be happy
In Heaven with you,
And Mommy can be happy
In my new house with me.
Happy birthday to Stevie,
Happy birthday to you.
I like happy birthdays . . .
Don't you?

September 22, 1993

37

Strength of Innocence

On Sunday, we go to church.
God is in our church,
And He is very special.
People pray to God,
So they can learn
To be special, too.
And then when their
Muscles-and-bones die,
They can go to Heaven
To be with Jamie.
Our church is made of brick.
That is special, too.
Very, very special.
Because now,
The big bad wolf
Can't blow the church down.

September 26, 1993

The Big Kids

Sometimes,
I wish I was five years old.
If I was five years old,
I would buy
White tennis shoes,
Like Emily,
Except she is
Only two years old.
I am three,
And on my next birthday,
I think I will try to
Turn into five years old,
And not four years old.
I would like to be five,
Because then I could
Ride a big bike,
And play soccer and football,
And go to kindergarten,
Like the Big Kids,
And I could say
Beavis-and-Butthead,
Like Christopher Dobbins.

October 2, 1993

38

If, and Then . . .

I will be a bumblebee.
If I could be a bumblebee,
I would fly.
If I could fly,
I would buzz.
If I could buzz and fly,
I would go to the store
And buy some
Milk and cookies.
Then, I would turn
Back into Mattie,
And eat them ALL up.

October 3, 1993

Leaf-Flowers

Now,
It is the fall.
And all of the
Leaves on the trees
Are turning into colors.
They are turning into orange,
Or yellow,
Or brown,
Or green,
Or red.
The leaves in my jungle
Will turn into so many colors.
And then,
They will float
Onto the ground.
I will put all of the
Yellow and brown and orange
Leaves into a pile,
And then I will jump
Into my pile of colors.
And the red ruby leaves
Will be my beautiful
Fall leaf-flowers.
I will put my leaf-flowers into
A cup of water,
Because they are very special.

October 6, 1993

Everything-but . . .

When my brother Jamie died,
Mommy put him in
A little white box.
His muscles-and-bones
Got buried, because they died.
He didn't need them anymore.
But what made Jamie happy
And special and loving,
Went to Heaven.
When Jamie got buried,
He had some very
Special things with him,
In the white box.
He had Mr. Bear and Binky,
He had his moose hat and
He had his moose blankie, and
He had his Blue Bunny Rabbit.
He had some other animals,
A Heaven cross, a flower . . .
Lots and lots of special things.
He also had a picture of me—
Mattie and Jamie together.
That's so special.
But,
Do you know what
He doesn't have?
He doesn't have real live me—
Mattie and Jamie together.

October 10, 1993

Brothers-the-Same, Brothers-Different

I have two teddy-bears.
One is Honey-Bear,
One is Birthday-Bear.
They are alike,
They are the same,
They are brothers.
Honey-Bear is yellow . . .
Birthday-Bear is yellow.
Honey-Bear has a tail . . .
Birthday-Bear has a tail.
I have a brother, Jamie.
We are alike,
We are the same,
Jamie had a trach . . .
I had a trach.
Jamie has my mommy . . .
I have my mommy.
But we are not alike,
And we are not the same.
Jamie has Mr. Bear . . .
But I have Mr. Bunny.
Jamie's body,
His muscles-and-bones died . . .
And I am a real live boy.

October 14, 1993

Housewarming

We moved into a new house.
It is a very nice new house.
I have a new bedroom,
And I have a jungle
In my new backyard.
I have a family room,
And a garage, and a kitchen,
And lots of other rooms.
We brought all of our
Clothes, and our toys, and
Our books, and our food, and
Our Jamie-box of memories,
To our new house.
Sometimes I wonder
If my older house misses us.
Maybe it is lonely.
Maybe we should send a
Postcard to our older house
In the mail.
I will say to my older house,
"Do you want to
Come to my new house?"
But my older house will say,
"No thanks, Mattie.
I think I'll just
Stay here in my grass,
And watch the airplanes.
But thank you for the postcard."
And my older house
Will not be sad anymore,
Because we remembered it.

                October 14, 1993

Healing the Hurt

The lab lady took my blood
Away from me today.
She let my mommy hold me,
And she stuck a needle
In me and took my red blood
Into a little glass jar.
Then she shook my blood up
In the little glass jar, and
Put a Snoopy-Dog bandage
On my arm.
My mommy
Made me feel better,
Because she held me,
And talked to me,
And loved me.
And the Snoopy-Dog bandage
Made me feel better,
Because I showed it to
The other children
In the waiting room.
They said, "Wow!"
I was proud.
But I was sad, too,
Because they still
Had to get their
Blood taken away from them.
Poor kids.
Poor friends.
I hope the lab lady
Has more Snoopy-Dog bandages,
And the kids have more mommies.

                October 28, 1993

41

Little Child, Big Fears

I have to go to the doctor's office today.
They will take a picture of my heart,
Because I think maybe it is broken.
My heart monitor and red-light machines
Beep a lot at nighttime,
And sometimes, I forget to breathe.
Sometimes, the doctor hurts me,
And sometimes, he doesn't hurt me.
Some doctors are my friends,
But it is always scary to see the doctor.
Even if I try not to cry,
I am still a little scared,
Or very, very scared.
Sometimes, the doctor lets me go home,
And sometimes, I have to stay in the hospital.
My mommy stays with me
When I am at the doctor's or the hospital,
And holds me and loves me.
But I remember when sometimes
The rules said she couldn't stay.
Then I was more scared,
Even when the doctor did not hurt me.
I do not like to be hurt.
I do not like to be scared.
But, I do not like to be broken.
Please fix me, doctor.
I don't want my muscles-and-bones to die,
Like my brother, Jamie.

October 27, 1993

42

Grief Anniversary

I tore pages out of the Mickey Mouse
Book at my school today
And I don't know why.
Jamie died today, last year,
And it was right after Halloween.
And now, Jamie isn't my brother.
He's Jesus' brother in Heaven.
And he's the little girl's and
The little boy's brother, too,
Because Katie and Stevie are
In Heaven with their brother, Jamie.
And I am here, alone.
And I am angry.
And I am sad.
And I am confused.
And I don't know why.
And I need to sit in my time-out chair,
And so does my mommy.
We need to sit in time-out together.
And I don't know why.
I don't know what we did, or why.
And I'm sorry.
I promise I am.
And I have tears coming
Out of my eyes,
And today is Jamie's Angel Day,
And I don't know why . . .

November 5, 1993

Early Heartsongs

Camera Shy

Today they took my
Picture at school.
I said to my mommy,
"I don't want them to
Take my picture at school.
School is my safe place."
But then my teacher
Showed me where they
Take pictures.
There was no big machine
That got rubbed on my belly.
There was no table that
Moved back and forth.
There were no wires that
Got glued on my head.
They didn't want to take
A picture of my heart,
Or of my chest,
Or of my head . . .
They wanted to take
A picture of ME!
My school IS safe,
So I smiled.

November 19, 1993

Empathy

Today,
I went with my mommy
To her doctor's office.
She had to wear an
Orange paper-dress,
And sit on the table
So the doctor could
Look at her.
I said to my mommy,
"You look beautiful!"
And my mommy smiled,
And then,
She was not scared
At the doctor's office.

November 22, 1993

Letter to Santa

Santa Claus,
Do you know what Church is
And why God is so good,
And why He made Heaven?
I know why.
I will tell you, Santa-Nicholas.
There is a something named
Church, that calls to
Every single person,
To come and pray all together
Or even all alone
In a special place,
And learn to be good listeners
To God and to each other.
And Church is so important
And God is so important
Because there will always
Be a place that remembers
Jamie the real live boy,
And then Jamie who died.
And there will always
Be a place that remembers
Every single person,
And Santa-Nicholas,
And even Mattie,
When I am a real live boy,
And then when I am died.
That's why Church is
So special, Santa.
That's why.

December 22, 1993

Fear

When I grow up
To be my brother, Jamie,
I will die
And go to Heaven.
Then my mommy
Will miss this Jamie, too.

December 27, 1993

Enough

I don't want
Santa Claus to die.
I don't want
Any more people to die.
I don't want
Any more children to die.
I don't want
Jamie to die.
I don't want
Danny to die.
I don't want
Katie or Stevie to die.
I don't want anyone
To die anymore!
Heaven
Is a wonderful place,
But when they die,
Matties are sad and angry
And want them
To come back, because
Here
Is a wonderful place, too.

December 27, 1993

Magic Merry-Go-Round

Now, we will have
A very special story.
It will be all about the
Magic Merry-Go-Round.
There are four horses
On this merry-go-round.
The Mattie-horse is
A Kid-Spaghetti-horse.
The Mommy-horse is
An All-American-horse.
The Friend-horse is
An Irish-Cockles-horse.
The Grandaddy-horse is
A Yellow-Russian-Racing-horse.
Those are the four horses.
They are all magic,
And they are on a
Magic Merry-Go-Round.
The reason that the
Horses are magic,
Is that they are all a family.
The reason that the
Merry-go-round is magic,
Is that it will never get broken,
So the magic horses
Will be a family,
Together Forever.

January 20, 1994

Night-Light Magic

Last night,
My mommy forgot
To turn on my night-light.
I was scared,
So I called her.
Mommy turned on the light,
And then she kissed me,
And tucked me in again.
And then,
I was a golden head
In the night.
That is when I'm a little boy,
Between an Angel,
And a Wild Thing.

January 24, 1994

Lesson of the Day

Everything is hard or soft.
Rocks and sliding boards,
They are hard.
Mr. Bunny and blankies,
They are soft.
And a hug?
The muscles-and-bones
Inside a hug are hard.
But the snuggles-and-love
Inside a hug are soft.

January 26, 1994

46

Act of Love, Act of Fear

My mommy has to use
Ow-ee-boo-boo walkers now.
They are called crutches.
That is because her
Muscles are very tired.
She might have to use a wheelchair,
Like I did,
Before I got my trach out,
Or like Jamie did,
Before he died.
My mommy is tired a lot.
She is a nice mommy.
But now,
Sometimes she is sad and angry,
And a little bit nasty,
Like Captain Hook.
Then she says,
"I'm sorry. I'm just very tired"
To Mattie who is Captain Hook.
Captain Hook needs a mommy
To save him.
But sometimes mommies are tired.
Captain Hook,
Who has Mattie hidden in his cape,
Loves his mommy.
So, he took off his
Captain Hook pirate hat,
And his cape, and his hook,
And then he put them on his mommy,
Because maybe,
His mommy needs a mommy, too.

February 13, 1994

47

Lesson of Love

Last night,
There were some scary things in bed with me.
There was a Captain.
I could see his one hand.
The other was hiding in his hook.
He was wearing a white shirt,
And a black coat-jacket,
And he was very mean and nasty.
There was a scary Shadow, too.
The Shadow was funny, but it was still scary.
There was the Nightmare from my closet.
It didn't take my Teddy like
The Nightmare in my attic,
But it was still scary, and a little nasty.
And, there was a Crocodile.
The Crocodile ate me all up.
I was all gone, and my mommy was so sad.
She missed me,
And she cried and wrote stories about me.
But I was not really all gone forever.
I was very nice.
I gave all those scary things lots of love,
And the Crocodile let me go.
Then, the Crocodile and
The Nightmare and the Shadow and the Captain
All left my bed.
They weren't scary and nasty to me anymore.
And that is because sometimes,
When something is mean and nasty,
It is just very sad and lonely and angry and confused,
And if you give it love, you can make it happy,
And then it will be nice.
And then, it will be able to love you back.

March 5, 1994

48

Taking a Joke

Sandy! Sandy!
Today is April Fool's Day!
And do you know what?
There is a
Big, green,
Giant elephant outside
Way up high in the tree!
Where?
Um, I don't see him either.
Mommy, where is that
Big, green, giant elephant
That you told me
To tell Sandy about?
April Fool's Day?
Oh, yeah!
I forgot . . .
Don't worry,
I was just "taking a joke," Sandy!

April 1, 1994

Officer Friendly

Our front porch is growing!
Help, help!
I need to dial the phone
And tell the police,
"Please, help!
Our front porch is growing!"
Then someone will
Knock at the front door.
Who is it?
It is the policeman.
And I will tell him again,
"Help, help!
Our front porch is growing!
Please, please, save my porch!
Turn it back into
A little porch."
And the policeman will
Turn the porch
Back into a little one.
He will say,
"Come look out the window.
See?"
The policeman
Saved my porch!
When he is all done,
I will say,
"Thank you!
Good bye!
I will see you next time,
When it grows again!"

April 5, 1994

49

Early Heartsongs

Excuse Class, 101

I don't want to go
To school today
Because I have chicken-pops.
I bought them at the store.
At the food store.
See?
Ock, bock, bock, bock.
And see,
They make my arms
Flap around like wings!
I need to
Stay home ALL week,
With my mommy.
And then,
And then I think
I will have the mumps.
And I will need to
Stay home all week again,
With my mommy some more!

May 3, 1994

The Art of Excuses

I have to clean up my mess
So I can eat my dinner.
And look at this mess!
There are
Sixteen dinosaurs!
I have to move
Sixteen dinosaurs
From the kitchen,
Back into the family room.
I don't know if I can do it.
Mommy says
I need to move all
Sixteen dinosaurs
Right now,
But I don't have
Sixteen hands!

May 5, 1994

In Search of a Birthday

Very soon,
In just two months,
It will be my birthday.
I will be four years old!
You see,
It is not my birthday, yet,
Because the clouds are low.
They're gray and puff-a-lee,
But that's why it's not my birthday yet.
They are May-clouds.
I need July-clouds.
And, if you are walking in the woods,
You need to be very careful.
Because if you see my birthday,
It could be very dangerous.
You might turn into four years old
Instead of me.
And I need to do that on July 17!
So, if you see my birthday,
Run, run, run the other way—
But tell me where you saw it, please,
So that I can go and find it!

May 18, 1994

The End of Forever

When I get bigger
And turn into five years old,
Like Jamie is now,
I will go to Heaven,
And bring him back.
When I get bigger
And turn into five years old,
I will tell Heaven,
"Sorry, you're not
Forever anymore."

May 26, 1994

The Forever-Wish

Sometimes,
I wish Heaven
Wasn't Forever.
Sometimes,
I wish Jamie
Could come back
From his
Forever-Heaven.
Sometimes,
I just miss him
So much,
That I can't even
Be happy,
Or sad,
Or angry.
I'm just alone,
Because that is a wish
That can't come true.

May 29, 1994

51

Early Heartsongs

Feeling to Feeling to Feeling, Minute to Minute to Minute

<u>8:00 a.m.</u>
I am going to die.
Everyone dies sometime.
Some people die when they are little children,
Like Jamie,
And like Katie and Stevie, and like Danny.
Some people die when they are grown up,
But I don't know anyone like that.
I am going to die.
Heaven is a very wonderful place,
And I will be very happy,
Like Jamie.
I don't want to be happy
Without Jamie anymore,
Even if I have a birthday party
Or a special treat.
Jamie is happy in Heaven.
Jamie's spirit is with us.
We can feel him, but
We can't touch him.
We can't see him, but
He can see us, and hear us.
I am happy with Mommy.
But sometimes I am not happy.
Sometimes I am angry or sad.
And sometimes I am scared
Mommy will die.
So I am going to die, and go to Heaven.
Mommy won't see me in Heaven,
But she can feel me,
Because my spirit will be with her.
And I will see and hear her
And be happy
Forever with Jamie.

52

8:10 a.m.
I think I am very afraid.
I just looked out the window,
And I think that
Something got into
My eye.
I saw something,
And it went into
My eye,
And now, maybe,
My eye will die.
I am afraid.
I don't want
My eye to die.
If it dies,
It will go to Heaven,
And I won't be able
To see it anymore.
And I won't be able
To see Mommy,
Either.
I am afraid.
I am afraid to blink.
I am afraid if I close
My eye, it will die
When I am not looking.
I can't blink.
I can't close my eye.
I won't let it die.
I want it to stay with me.

8:15 a.m.
In Church, I heard that
People who listen and
Do good things,
Go to Heaven.
Heaven is a wonderful place,
And it is with
God and Jamie.
But I don't want to
Go to Heaven, yet.
Maybe,
If I don't do good listening,
I won't have to die.

June 9, 1994

53

Early Heartsongs

Bumpy Feet

Sometimes,
I forget to breathe,
And the alarm on my
Heart monitor beeps at me.
And sometimes,
I don't forget to breathe.
I just can't breathe.
I cough and cough.
And my heart hurts.
I am a little bit afraid.
Maybe my
Muscles-and-bones
Will not work anymore,
And I will die.
When you die,
You don't breathe anymore.
You can't breathe anymore.
I try to breathe,
But I only cough and cough.
And then it makes
My feet bumpy.
See?

When I sit in my rocking chair
And try to breathe
And I am only coughing,
Then my feet
Bump on the floor.
And when I cough a lot,
Then they bump a lot.
And then,
My feet get a headache.
Today,
My feet have a headache,
And my chest has a heartache,
And I am a little bit
Afraid and worried.
I think I need
Someone else to
Hold me and rock me,
So my feet don't bump.
And then, maybe,
My heart won't die.

June 12, 1994

54

The Tangle-Monster's Joke

Every night,
My mommy puts on
My heart monitor patches,
And she wraps a special belt
Around my tummy.
All of my wires and
My oxygen tubes
Go into the belt.
Then, she tucks me into bed,
And I close my eyes
And I fall to sleep.
But while I am asleep,
Even when I am
Having pleasant dreams,
The Tangle-Monster comes!
He rolls me
Around in my bed,
This way and that way and
Here and there and
Up and down and
All around . . .
When I wake up, I know
The Tangle-Monster
Was there,
Because all of my wires and
My oxygen tubes
Are all tangled up
Around my legs and
Around my arms and
Around my tummy and
Around my bed!
Mommy says,
"Oh, bother!

That old Tangle-Monster
Was here last night!"
Well, last night,
I said the Magic Words,
And told the Tangle-Monster
"Don't come near
My bed tonight!"
Then I put
Tangle-Monster bait
All over my room
And in my closet,
So I could
Catch him if he came!
I closed my eyes and
I fell to sleep.
And do you know what
Happened when I woke up?
The bait was still there!
The Magic Words worked!
The Tangle-Monster
Did not come!
But do you know what else?
I was still all tangled up!
I said, "How did this happen?"
And then, I figured it out.
The Tangle-Monster
Got his friend,
The Shadow-on-the-Wall,
To come to my room
And tangle me all up for him!
What a silly joke he played!

June 17, 1994

56

Heaven's Eyes

I have blue eyes,
Just like my brother, Jamie,
And just like my
Other brother and sister,
Stevie and Katie,
And just like Heaven.
Heaven has blue eyes.
Maybe.
My favorite colors are
Pink and orange.
So maybe,
Heaven has
Pink and orange eyes, too.

June 18, 1994

Importance of Rainbows

Mattie is a nice boy.
He will never call
His mommy "yo-yo."
He will call her
"My rainbow"
Because rainbows
Are so special
And beautiful,
And make you happy
After the storm.

June 20, 1994

So Many Angels

Actually,
I am a very
Lucky Real Live Boy.
I know so many Angels.
My brother, Jamie
Is an Angel.
My brother, Stevie
Is an Angel.
My sister, Katie
Is an Angel.
My friend, Danny
Is an Angel.
And I think, maybe,
My friend, Jesus
Is an Angel.
Wow!
That makes
So many Angels.
It is sad
To be a
Lucky Real Live Boy
And know
All of these Angels.
But it is special
To know them, too.

June 21, 1994

57

Love Letter

Violets are red, and violets are blue,
And violets are orange and pink
And purple and brown.
And thank You, God, for the
Beautiful violets,
And thank You, God,
For my teachers and my friends,
And my mommy and my world,
And for everything and everyone.
I love You, God.

June 22, 1994

Festive Heartsongs

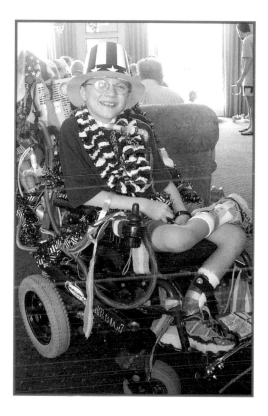

Memories are a gift of the past,
That we hold in the present,
To create what can be a great future.
Treasure and keep memories,
For the sake of Life.

Excerpt from "About Memories" by Mattie J.T. Stepanek,
in *Celebrate Through Heartsongs* (Hyperion/VSP, 2002)

PREVIOUS PAGE: Mattie celebrates the Fourth of July, 2003

TOP: Harley-Davidson "Biker Mattie," Halloween 1999

BOTTOM LEFT: Mattie the Head-Elf hugging Santa on the Fantasy Flight, December 1997

BOTTOM RIGHT: Mattie at a pumpkin farm, fall 1998

This first time I met Mattie Stepanek, I was onstage doing a sound check. It wasn't going smoothly and some of the musicians were acting out inappropriately. Mattie and Jeni were side stage, and having just met them, I was quite embarrassed. I walked over and apologized saying, "I'm sorry, they're acting like children," to which Mattie replied, with his signature smile, "I resent that remark!" That was when I knew I had made a new friend.

The following September, Jeni and Mattie came out to California for the MDA telethon. We went to Disneyland (Mattie had never been). Because of Mattie's dependence on his ventilator, he could only be disconnected from the life support equipment on his wheelchair for a total of 20 minutes a day. He had to decide which rides to go on. Mattie embraced this challenge with his typical enthusiasm. He did not see his dilemma as being all the rides he would miss out on, but basked in the freedom to experience a few. (FYI: Mattie's first choice was Star Tours.)

That vacation, like so many other special and simple times my family and I shared with Mattie, is a memory we will cherish forever. Making memories was one of the things that kept Mattie going. He loved people and doing stuff. He was a poet and a philosopher, but he was also a kid, and his affection for everyday things was infectious. He loved his family, his friends, his dog Micah, music, movies, video games, playing games, and eating crabs on his birthday. He loved making his mom coffee in the morning.

For myself, as an artist, Mattie will forever inspire me. As a person, he taught me to see every day as a gift. The humbling reality of Mattie's struggle was a life lesson in itself, but his kindness, insight, compassion for others, and his love of life is the elixir for what ails us. He talked about wanting to have seven children, all the while knowing it was an unrealistic hope. However, his life was built on hopes and dreams: hope to live another day, the dream of another sunset, and, especially, hope for peace in the world. This is my friend, Mattie Stepanek.

—Christopher Cross

(Grammy and Oscar Award-Winning Musician and Artist)

Excerpt from Tribute by Christopher Cross (May 2005)

61

*C*elebrating life every day in some way truly mattered to Mattie. Of course there were holidays—religious, commemorative, or just for fun—which delighted him and became the root of many poems. And, clearly, he treasured the daily gifts of nature and memories and angels. But Mattie also found reason to rejoice in annual cycles and events, like the first and last days of school, and summer camp and vacations. He was equally enthralled with ordinary occurrences embedded in the passing of time and seasons, like sunrises and sunsets, thunder clouds and autumn leaves, spring blossoms and early winter snow flurries. Mattie rarely missed an opportunity to playfully howl under a full moon, or don one of his four costumes and assume the role of Season King.

Like most people faced with immense physical and emotional challenges, Mattie had moments when he asked the inevitable question, "Why me?" But he never got lost in this unanswerable domain. Instead, Mattie would consider the issue, "Who else would I choose to give this life?" and come to the conclusive statement, "Why not me?" Then, he would move on to the more manageable issues of how to continue appreciating and relishing life as it unfolded for him.

We creatively problem-solved how to safely bring liquid oxygen tanks out onto the beach, so that he could listen to whales and watch dolphins while awaiting the first pale streaks of dawn rising across the ocean. We contemplated the possibilities of each day's schedule, so that he could optimize his activities during the one or two ten-minute periods he might be able to handle off of his life-support system. When he could no longer breathe without the ventilator, even for a brief period, and when he spent almost or every moment living in the intensive care unit, Mattie still found motivation and means for living life festively.

This chapter, Festive Heartsongs, takes the reader through a year of celebrations as Mattie captures them in poetic form. He transforms thoughts and reactions into words and reflections that echo his love for all aspects of life. Through these poems, we are reminded of the important matter of being optimistic, resilient, even joyful during times of adversity, and we are gifted, again, with his perpetual message of hope and peace.

Festive Heartsongs

IAFF Softball Tournament

I didn't hit a home run.
I didn't even swing a bat.
I didn't catch a high-fly ball.
I didn't even catch a low foul ball.
I didn't have a position on the field.
I didn't even play for a single team.
And probably, I won't ever
Be able to do any of those things.
But . . .
I supported every team.
I cheered whether they won or lost.
I gave hugs to all the players and people.
I raised MDA funds using my super-soaker
And writing my "Luck for a Buck" messages.
I shared my Heartsong,
Making friends with everyone!
And then, I won—
"Individual Player Sportsmanship Award!"
    . . . The most spiritual and best award
        In the tournament, and
            In my life!

September 13, 1998

63

How the Snows Come and Go

In the spring, the meadows
Are like pretty houses
Filled with flowers and colors.
Pink and red, and blue and
White, and orange and
Yellow, and all the other
Colors of the warm spring.
In the summer, the grass joins
The flowers in the meadows.
The little tiny green grass
Of the spring grows into
Tall summer grasses
And blows back and forth in the
Warm breezes that help us
Smell the flowers of spring
And then summer.
In the fall, the leaves drop
From their trees to the ground.
They turn all the autumn colors,
And then fall,
Peacefully, and quietly, and
Sometimes, a little bit noisy.
Sometimes, the leaves fall
Like a big, warm
Feather to the ground, or
Like a middle-sized feather, or
Like a tiny-sized feather.
And sometimes,
The leaves fall in a storm
Like feathers
Exploding in a pillow fight.

On the last day of fall, maybe
It rains, and maybe it doesn't.
Still, we smell the leaves of fall,
And then, the winter coming.
In the winter, we can smell
The cold and the ice
Even before we see it.
Maybe it will rain some more,
But it will get colder and colder,
And the rain will turn icy,
And then, rain into snow.
Sometimes the snow falls
Onto warm ground.
Sometimes the snow falls
Onto cold ground, like
Icy-white feathers, so soft to
Fall into and play with,
And even to eat.
And then, the last day
Of the January snow comes,
And on the Saturday, there is
Still snow on the ground.
But the snow melts into ice,
And into yellow and gray . . .
And we don't want to eat it
Or even touch it anymore.
That is how the winter snow
Comes, and that is how the
Winter snow ends, and that is
Also the end of my story
About the winter snows.

January 9, 1996

64

Visions of Voices

Mommy,
You know what?
One day,
When my friend was
Still visiting,
After it rained
I saw a rainbow.
And all the colors
Were so beautiful.
And you know what?
This rainbow came
On a blue sky!
There was only one
Little spot of gray
Behind the rainbow.
And under the rainbow,
There were
Katie and Stevie and Jamie.

I saw their voices.
And their voices looked
Just exactly the way
That they talked!
They didn't say anything—
Their voices just smiled
And after about a minute,
They disappeared again
From under the rainbow.
I was so happy
To see these voices.
And it didn't even
Have to be gray!
And you know what?
I'll never forget this.
I'll never forget it.

February 1, 1995

Mommy Mine, My Valentine
(to the tune of "Clementine")

Oh, my mommy
Won't you be mine
On this day of Valentine?
You're my sweetheart
You're my darlin',
You're my cloud nine's silver line.

I think Cupid
And his arrow
Have put love into my heart,
And to you now
I shall deep bow
To say, "Juliet, where thou art?"

Don't forget that
Valentine's Day
Isn't only a day to play,
It's the feast day
Of St. Valentine
And we all really should pray.

Oh, my mommy
Won't you be mine
On this day of Valentine?
You're my sweetheart
You're my darlin',
You're my cloud nine's silver line.

Happy Valentine's Day!
Love, Your Son,
Mattie Joseph Thaddeus Stepanek

February 14, 2000

Birthday Words to Everland

Today is Jamie's birthday.
Happy Birthday, Jamie.
Neverland makes you forget,
But I didn't forget you.
I promise.
Really I do.
We had chocolate cake
With a "5" on it,
And we sang
"Happy Birthday" to you
So you will have
A happy birthday in Heaven.
I love you, Jamie.
You are my brother.
I won't forget you,
Not even in Neverland.

February 9, 1994

About Easter Time

Easter is a long time away.
It comes when
The rains come,
Because that is when
New things grow,
And we have
New life,
Just like in Heaven.

February 27, 1994

The Spirit of Success

It is the spirit that makes school a success.
The spirit goes through different seasons,
And traveling through each season takes time.
During this time, many experiences
Affect the mind, and the heart,
And the essence of our being.
These experiences are shaped by people—
Our teachers, our friends, and our families.
Our spirits are gently, yet meaningfully
Touched, as we learn from these people.
And through these lessons,
We build our future, and our life,
As we grow in the spirit of success.

June 13, 1999

Lessons of MDA Camp

I learned to take a shower.
I learned to love nature.
I learned to crab, and
Fish, and row a canoe.
I helped Cody want to
Brush his teeth.
I made lots of friends.
My counselor
Cried when I left.
I got away from the
Stress in my life.
I learned I matter,
To lots of people, and
That I'm a really cool kid.

June 27, 1998

Summer Magic

There were so many people
At Watkins Park . . .
I could hear the roar of
Children, before I got
On the playground.
The wind tickled my tummy
As I flew forward on the swing.
I made a new friend, Malik,
And together,
We climbed, and slid,
And jumped, and hid,
On all the equipment
At the Park.
Having so much fun
With my new friend,
I didn't even remember
How very hot it was.

July 10, 1998

68

Favorite Things

Hooray! Hooray!
I'm five years old today!
At last I'm five,
At last I'm five,
Hooray for me today!
I've always wanted to be
Five years old.
Five is my favorite number,
Just like left is my
Favorite hand and my
Favorite foot,
And just like
Feathers and leaves and
Sticks and butterflies and
Seashells and shiny jewels
Are my favorite
Treasure things,
And just like pink and orange
And brown and gray
Are my favorite colors,
And just like people
And sunsets and rainbows
Are my favorite gifts
From God and the Angels!

And do you know what else
Makes today so special?
God gave me my very own
Pink and orange sunrise
Because it was my birthday!
It was my favorite color mix
And there was lots of gray fog
All over the hills and trees
And it was for me because
It is my birthday and
It is my sister's Angel Day!
I'm such a lucky little boy
To be five years old
With my very own sunrise.
And now that I'm five,
And I've used up all
The fingers on one hand,
Well, that makes me
So close to ten years old,
Which will be my next
Favorite number and
Favorite birthday!

July 17, 1995

69

What to Do . . .

What to do,
What to do,
At the beach,
Just what to do . . .
Swim in the ocean.
Collect some shells.
Dig for pirate treasure.
Study jellyfish.
Play games, ride rides.
Meet new people.
So much to do,
So much to do,
At the beach,
Just so much to do . . .

August 17, 1997

Message in the Sand

If I could write a special
Message in the sand,
I would write—
"Have a special sea-day!"
And "See the sea!"
I would want the world
To know "Be peaceful!"
And "Be happy!" and
"Remember all your dreams!"

August 19, 1997

New School Year

Tonight is the night to dream about
Apples, and pencils, and books.
Why would we dream about these things?
Because tonight is a very special night . . .
It is New School-Year's Eve,
And all the teachers, boys, and girls
Are about to have fun on
New School-Year's Day!
Tomorrow, we will begin new lessons
In math, and reading, and maybe even science.
(I really shouldn't mention about
Recess, center time, and lunch,
But everyone knows how much fun they are, too.)
In this new year, I hope to have old friends,
And a little bit of new friends also,
But I hope we don't have so many kids
That we all get smooshed together
When we work and play!
So, it is time to say good-night, sweet dreams,
And may we all have a great New School-Year!

September 1, 1997

Pre-Sense

When the first breath
Of frost hangs
Like mist in the air,
When the crisped leaves
Are swirling
And crunched everywhere,
When the dark sets
In longer
And pumpkins are seen . . .
Then we know that
So soon it
Will be Halloween!

         September 24, 1998

Macabre Term

Fall winds howl
Like ghoblins
Seeking lost sheets.
Fall shadows lurk
Like zombies'
Stretched-out limbs.
Fall colors haunt
Like yellowed photos
Of those who have
Returned to dust.

         October 31, 1999

About Halloween Costumes

When I was a baby
I was an Astronaut and
Jamie was a Pilot, and
Together we reached
For Heaven and the stars.
When I was one
I was a Cowboy and
Jamie was a Pumpkin.
I rode my horsie and
He lay on the couch.
When I was two
I was a Wild Thing and
Jamie was a Moose, because
Those were our favorite things.
When I was three
I was Pinocchio,
Because I wondered why
The Blue Fairy sometimes let
Little boys live again, and
Sometimes, they stayed dead.
When I was four I was the
Wicked Warlock of the West,
Because I was angry
That my brother died.
I wanted the Wizard of Oz
To bring him home.
When I was five
I was the Grinch
Because I was angry
And hurt about many things.
When I was six
I was a Royal Knight,
Because I wanted to fight back,

And I believed good
Could overcome that evil.
When I was seven
We had finally moved away
And I was a Wizard
Because I wanted
Things to magically get better.
Now, I am eight and
I will be Oscar the Grouch
Because I just want to forget
All the pain and sadness
Of my growing up.
The trash can
Is my armor against grief.
I want to forget
Anger and fear and violence.
I want to be little, and have
My mommy protect me again.
I just want to be a kid.
I just want to have fun
And have my Heartsong
Be clear and strong again.
Next year,
I will grow up again, and
Who knows what I will be.
I might have the Force and
Be a Jedi Knight, or wear the
White Robe of Gandalf.
Finally, the good could, and
Would, win over the evil.
I might be something,
But I don't know.
It all depends
On what happens in my life.

October 23, 1998

73

Thanksgiving Prayer

Dear God,
Let us be thankful for our material things in life:
      Good food, our jobs, safe houses,
      Clothing, and our prized belongings.
Let us be even more thankful for our lives:
      The ability to have our friends
      And family together today
      To celebrate Thanksgiving,
      And to celebrate all other days.
Let us be most thankful for You, God,
      And for Your grace.
Let us be ever thankful for Heaven,
      So that after our life on earth,
      We may have eternity with God,
      And with all those
      Who have gone before us,
      And with all those who will
      Enter the Kingdom after us.
Dear God,
Let us be truly thankful
      For the gift of each new day.
      Help us to live thankfully throughout the year,
      So that when our time comes for the gift of Eternity,
      The eternal echo of our life here on earth
      Will be a song of goodness worth remembering.
We ask these things in Your name
      On this Thanksgiving Day.
Amen.

November 23, 2000

Fantasy Flight 9700:
The Best Trip Ever

Dear Santa,
I know you are so close to God,
You are such a good person,
And you live so close to Heaven
Up on the North Pole.
Thank you for inviting me
To your home again this year . . .
It was the best trip ever!
I was five years old
The first year I flew there.
I wished for Legos,
But I didn't tell you that.
I asked you to please visit my
Brothers and sister in Heaven,
And that would be my gift.
And even though I never
Said it out loud,
You gave me a big bag,
With a huge box of Legos.
When I was six years old,
I wished I could be one of
Your Elves and help others.
You said you'd work on it, and
You gave me the greatest
Stuffed monkey, Beedey.
I was afraid he would die
Because he has a disability,
But we are still alive, and
We're back visiting you again!
Now, I have grown
Into seven years old.
One of your grown-up helpers
Gave me an Elf-vest and hat,
And a name badge that said,

"Mattie—Elf in Training."
You remembered my wish, Santa,
And you made it come true.
I was so excited to work for you.
Next year, I will be a Real-Elf!
You have given me everything
I've asked for, even in silence!
This year, I am asking you for
Something very difficult.
This year's Christmas wish
Is for peace and safety.
A lot of bad things
Have been happening lately.
I'm afraid for my mom and me.
I'm afraid for our country and
I'm very afraid for our world.
I promise I will never ask you
For another toy, if you can
Just give us peace and safety.
I don't want to die from my
Mitochondrial myopathy,
And I don't want to die
Because someone gets angry.
I will work hard for you, Santa,
So please keep us safe, and
Please give us peace.
Maybe, since I'm an Elf, my
Mom and I could just come to
The North Pole to live with you.
You'd be a great daddy, Santa.
I love you, and you love me.
From, Mattie Stepanek

December 6, 1997

Enter the Season

The season is upon us now,
Let us enter, here is how . . .

Come in joy to celebrate.
Come in hope for future's sake.
Come in gently, open-hearted.
Come for unborn, and departed.
Come in happiness and mirth.
Come with faith that serves the earth.
Come in kindness, come forgiving.
Come to share the gift of living.
Come in patient, calm, assuring.
Come with grace and trust enduring.
But most of all, let's come in peace,
The dark of angry hurt, release.

The season 'tis upon us now,
As we enter, let us vow . . .

For young and old in every land,
Let us come joined hand-in-hand.

December 10, 2000

Winter Fun

Every December 21st,
The winter fun begins
Because that's when
I become the Snow-King!
When I was younger,
Auntie Flora helped
Me make my costume.
I have an icicle necklace,
A silver snow crown, and
A golden scepter with gems
And a snowflake on the end.
As the Snow-King,
I make up poems and stories
About winter fun.
I also build snow forts
With Uncle Paw, and
Play in the snow with Mommy.
The midnight of fall is coming,
And soon winter will dawn.
And I, the Snow-King, will say:
"Let the winter fun begin!"

December 16, 1998

The Twelve Lights of Christmas

Light the first light of Christmas for thankfulness and prayer . . .
And everything you see and hear and feel and do.
Light the second light of Christmas for happiness and joy . . .
And be cheerful with everyday and everyone around.
Light the third light of Christmas for colors and music . . .
Gifts in people, gifts for people, gifts everywhere from God.
Light the fourth light of Christmas for thoughtfulness and love . . .
And be gentle and kind to all God's people and animals.
Light the fifth light of Christmas for mercy . . .
So we can be forgiving and forgiving like our God.
Light the sixth light of Christmas for all miracles . . .
Like babies and Jesus and things
That happen like magic, but they're not.
Light the seventh light of Christmas for understanding . . .
So we can have peace inside ourselves and all around the world.
Light the eighth light of Christmas for our Earth . . .
It's the only planet where humans can survive.
Light the ninth light of Christmas for Heaven and Angels . . .
We can keep them all around us, everywhere, with goodness.
Light the tenth light of Christmas for life . . .
No matter how short or long it is,
It's a wonderful blessing from God.
Light the eleventh light of Christmas for spirit . . .
The strongest part of us that rises out of death forever.
Light the twelfth light of Christmas for Heartsongs . . .
The glow inside of us that keeps the Light of Christmas bright.
And when our hearts glow with the Lights of Christmas,
We will remember spirit and life and Heaven and Angels,
And Earth and understanding and miracles and mercy,
And thoughtfulness and love and colors and music,
And happiness and joy and thankfulness and prayer . . .
And become better people throughout the whole, entire year.

December 10, 1996

Decoration Celebration

Christmas lights twinkle and glow all around.
Sometimes, houses have lots of decorations outside.
Sometimes, we can see a beautiful tree through a window.
Sometimes, only one candle shines from a home.
But I understand now, about the lights of Christmas.
I used to think that people who put lots and lots
Of lights and decorations on their house were
The ones who loved God and Christmas the most.
I used to think that a bright house meant
That holy and good people lived inside.
I used to think that houses with just a single candle,
Or with no decorations at all, meant that
Scrooge people lived there, who didn't celebrate the Lord.
Now, I am older.
Now, I am wiser.
Now, I understand
That Jesus is the true Light of the World.
When we decorate for Christmas,
We are showing signs of friendship with God,
And with others by inviting them to share our Light.
Some people don't have a lot of money for
Lights and decorations, but they have good hearts,
And they celebrate with prayer and kindness.
I love to look at all of the Christmas lights,
But I know not to judge about people
By how their house looks outside,
Because it's what's inside that really matters.
The Light of the World is Jesus,
So we must shine from our hearts for Him.
Then, even if we don't have the money to decorate,
Santa will see the brightness of our home, and
He'll know where to stop in the dark of the night.

December 25, 1997

78

Ms. Santa Claus

Holiday cheer
Lasts all year,
But at Christmastime the most.
Symbols of seasons
Have many reasons, though
Santa's being seems winter's host.
Jolly Santa Claus'
Tradition
Is a favorite for little kids,
They see a red suit,
White heard, black boots,
And eyes with a twinkle within.
This year I have been skeptical
If Santa Claus is real,
But now I know the spirit is
And the red suit's for appeal.
My mom takes such good care of me,
She taught me to believe,
But she's my Secret Santa,
My presents she achieves.
The greatest Kringle of them all,
My mom's my best Christmas present.
She makes my life a special gift,
Each daily celebration pleasant.

Merry Christmas, Mommy!
Love, Your Elf,
Mattie

December 25, 2001

Perhaps, We Could . . .

Perhaps we could . . .
Let the reason for this season
Live throughout
The coming year,
Let this season be the reason
To dispel all
Hate and fear.
Let each reason for our season
Unite us
In one voice,
Let this season be
Our reason to make
Hope and peace our choice.

Perhaps we share
In Kwanzaa,
Perhaps on
Christmas Day,
Perhaps with
Lighted candles
During Hanukkah
We pray.
Perhaps we practice
Ramadan,
Perhaps we
Meditate,
Perhaps we praise
In other ways
Or just believe
In fate.

Perhaps we do
Not worship,
Perhaps we
Grace alone,
Perhaps it
Doesn't matter
Since true Faith
Cannot be known.
Perhaps we could
Join voices,
Perhaps we could
Join hands,
Perhaps we could
Join peacefully
Our hearts
In all the lands.

Perhaps we could . . .
Let the reason for this season
Live throughout
The coming year,
Let this season be the reason
To dispel all
Hate and fear.
Let each reason for our season
Unite us
In one voice,
Let this season be
Our reason to make
Hope and peace our choice.

Festive Heartsongs

Perhaps we wish
For harmony,
Perhaps we strive
For paz,
Perhaps we want
Tranquility
Or call out
For spokoj.
Perhaps we gently
State shalom,
Perhaps we pray
For fred,
Perhaps amani
Or hoa binh
Or truce
Is what is said.

Perhaps we speak
Of amity,
Perhaps we seek
Repose,
Perhaps we pledge
Neutrality
Or pace
For our foes.
Perhaps we yearn
For kai lug,
Perhaps for
War to cease,
Perhaps
It doesn't matter
If our faith just
Leads to peace.

Perhaps we could . . .
Let the reason for this season
Live throughout
The coming year,
Let this season be the reason
To dispel all
Hate and fear.
Let each reason for our seasons
Unite us
In one voice,
Let this season be
Our reasons to make
Hope and peace our choice.

Perhaps, we could . . .
Let the reason for this season
Live throughout the coming year.
Perhaps, we could . . .
Let this season be the reason
To rise above all fear.
Perhaps, we could . . .
Let each reason for our season
Unite us in One Voice.
Perhaps, we should . . .
Let this season be
Our reason to make
Hope and peace our choice.

December 25, 2002

81

Angel-Family

One day,
God will say,
"Yes, Mattie,
It's your turn to come into Heaven."
And when I die,
You must bury me
With Geco, my Hawaiian toy lizard.
Then, you must buy a new one
And put it under the Christmas tree
Every year.
You must pray to me,
And I will smile with you
And come around to you with
My Angel-wings.
And then,
When God says that
It's your turn, Mommy,
You will die, and
You will come with me into
The Everything and Everywhere of Heaven.
You will see me then,
And Katie and Stevie and Jamie, too.
Just imagine!
All of us together again,
Joined with God!
Wow!
We will be the happiest Angel-Family!

January 14, 1995

Festive Heartsongs

Stormy Heartsongs

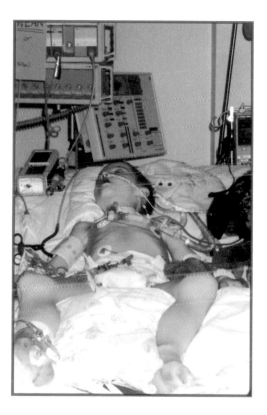

Sometimes,
I feel like I have
Broken through
The wall into the
Land of Loneliness.
I cry in my mind, and
I cry in my heart, but
I never cry in my eyes . . .

Excerpt from "Land of Loneliness" by Mattie J.T. Stepanek,
in *Hope Through Heartsongs* (Hyperion/VSP, 2002)

PREVIOUS PAGE: Mattie, critically ill and in a coma, spring 2001

TOP: Mattie at Ground Zero, World Trade Center site, February 2002

BOTTOM LEFT: Mattie comforts his brother, Jamie, March 1992

BOTTOM RIGHT: Mattie as the Wicked Warlock of the West, Halloween 1994

When I was running for governor a number of years ago, my wife and I didn't have much money so we traveled around the state and we estimated later that we shook hands personally with 600,000 people. Later I ran for president, as some of you may remember, and campaigned in all fifty states. Subsequently, I traveled around the world. In fact, since I left the White House, my wife and I have been to more than 120 nations. And we have known kings and queens, and we've known presidents and prime ministers, but the most extraordinary person whom I have ever known in my life is Mattie Stepanek. . . .

We were close enough for Mattie to share some of his problems with me in his private [e-mail] messages. He talked about when he and Jeni were not well off and some local [organizations] would take up a food collection and send it to them. Mattie used to examine the labels on the food and quite often he said he would find that the date had expired and that people were giving poor people inferior food that they didn't want to use themselves. And Mattie said, "If my books make a lot of money, we're going to get food that's brand new and make sure that poor people get the best food, even if we have to eat the old, outdated food in our house." He was very proud of the fact that he and his mother could move into a place that had windows.

Mattie said he wanted to be, as an ultimate goal in his life, an ambassador of humanity and a daddy. . . . Mattie was deeply aware of international affairs and shared a lot of his thoughts with me. He was once again in the intensive care unit when the war in Iraq began, and Mattie burst into uncontrollable sobs of grief and anger. Jeni said he had never cried nearly so much about his own health or his own problems. He wrote me right after that and I will quote exactly what he said: "Dear Jimmy, I am hurting about the war and I cried last night when I saw the attack on Iraq. I am not trying to be disrespectful, but I feel like [the] decision was made long ago that [we were] going to have this war. Imagine [spending] as much time and energy considering the possibility of peace . . . as convincing others of the inevitability of war. We'd be at a different point in history today."

Mattie was obviously extremely idealistic, but not completely idealistic. He also wrote me in a subsequent letter, "I know that I should be peaceful with everyone, but it's also not smart," he said, "to put yourself in a dangerous situation. Like even though I would want to talk to Osama bin Laden about peace in the future, I wouldn't want to be alone with him in his cave."

85

In the same letter he asked me if I would join him not just in that meeting, but in writing a book that Mattie wanted to call, and had already named, Just Peace. *In an incredible way for a child his age, he analyzed the semantics of the words "just" and "peace." . . . Poetry seemed to flow out of Mattie, kind of like an automatic stream, directed by inspiration through Mattie's hands for the enjoyment of hundreds of thousands, maybe millions of people . . . He combined humor with serious thoughts. All of [his poems] I would say are unique, surprising when you read them. . . .*

It's hard to know anyone who has suffered more than Mattie. Sandy [Newcomb, a dear family friend] sent us almost daily reports about his bleeding, internally and from his fingers. I doubt that anyone in this great auditorium has ever suffered so much except his mother Jeni, and our Savior Jesus Christ, who is also here with us today. I always saw the dichotomy between Mattie as a child and with the characteristics and intelligence and awareness of an adult. He was concerned about his legacy, wanting to have seven children and talking about his grandchildren, but Mattie's legacy is forever because his Heartsongs will resonate in the hearts of people forever . . .

—Former President Jimmy Carter
(Nobel Peace Prize Laureate)

◆

lthough Mattie truly appreciated and celebrated the gift of life, there were many storms during his brief "almost fourteen" years. Mattie intimately knew the pain of loss and grief through the deaths of his siblings, hospital roommates, and other friends with disabilities, and as he coped with the nearing certainty of his own mortality. He also weathered the effects of his mother's divorce, financial poverty, and the unfortunate but too-common teasing and alienation often experienced by children who have disabilities. Most of all, Mattie was greatly distressed by the reality of emotional and physical violence, and the existence of war.

In this chapter, Stormy Heartsongs, readers learn why Mattie recognized very early in his years that life was "short, sweet, and sacred." These poems, which span a decade of writing, explore questions and convictions that shaped Mattie's understanding of peace, for individuals and for the world. And they portray the reflections of one child, one young man, one human being, with the desire to become a peacemaker.

Excerpts from Eulogy by Jimmy Carter during funeral of Mattie J.T. Stepanek, June 28, 2004, Wheaton, Maryland

86

Stormy Heartsongs

Revelation

As the planets revolve
Around the sun,
So, too,
Do my fears revolve
Around a memory.
As the stars twinkle
On the outside
But are on fire inside,
So, too,
Do I shine
With fiery dread
Of what might happen.
As the Lord trusted our
Creator to not forsake Him,
So, too,
Do I put my faith in God,
My real Father and protector.

October 9, 1999

Two Weeks of Rememberies

I will cry when
Amanda goes back home.
I love my cousin.
I love my brother,
And my other brother
And my sister,
But they died,
And they can't be here
For me to touch.
And now, my cousin
Will not be here either.
That is just so sad.
Everyone keeps going away.
All the little children
That I love keep dying
Or moving or leaving.
So, I will cry.
But, only a little bit
Because then I will feel better,
And I will remember
My rememberies,
And only be sad sometimes.

August 21, 1994

Anniversary Reaction

Today is a dying day.
I'm afraid if Lissa goes
Away into her house,
I'll never see her again.
I'm afraid if I
Close my eyes,
I'll stop breathing and
Never wake up again.
I'm afraid
I am very sad,
Because I miss Jamie
So much, and
Today is a dying day,
Isn't it?
And that makes me
Angry and sad,
And it makes me
Afraid, too.

November 5, 1995

Little Tin Man

I need another heart.
A testimonial.
A watch-heart that ticks.
So that if I cry,
Or if I die,
My heart is still there,
And I can still move,
And maybe come back to life.

July 8, 1994

Not Everything Grows

Raffi says
That everything
Grows and grows.
Raffi says
Mothers do and fathers do,
And he says
Sisters do and brothers do.
My mommy and
My friends grow.
And I grow, too.
But sisters and brothers
Don't always grow.
My sister and brothers died.
Their muscles-and-bones
Don't work anymore at all,
So, they don't grow and grow.
I like your music, Raffi,
But you made a mistake.

July 2, 1994

The Wish

Sometimes,
I wish Jamie
Had looked up
At us from his bed,
And said,
"I won't die.
I promise.
Everything will be alright.
Don't worry."
But,
He didn't.
And he did die.
And sometimes,
Everything is not alright.

January 19, 1994

89

True, True Empathy

I miss Danny,
Just like I miss Jamie.
Danny is in Heaven
With his cups now.
He is not cold anymore,
Because he is in Heaven.
He is happy, but I miss him.
And Julie and Jessie will miss
Him because they don't have
A brother here anymore.
I had a brother here with me,
And he died.
They had a brother with them,
And he died.
Now, they are Heaven-Brothers.
Julie and Jessie will be
Sad and angry and confused.
They will stomp their feet
And cry and cry.
I will hug them and hold them,
And I will talk to them
About Danny.
I will remember him
And his cups
And his noises
And his walking
With Julie and Jessie.
Then, after they cry,
And talk about Danny,
They can be happy again,
Sometimes.

December 27, 1993

Magic Mirror, Real Visions

When I pretend to be the Beast,
I have a magical mirror.
The Beast can look into it and
See whatever he wishes to see.
So I say, "I want to see
My brother, please!"
And the mirror could let me
See Jamie again.
The real live Jamie.
And I'd want to see something
I've never seen before—
Katie and Stevie,
My sister and other brother.
That is such a lovely
Pretend wish.
And perhaps, someday,
I'll have a real
Magic mirror of my own.
And when all of the
Days of pretend have ended,
I can really see
My brother, again.

February 16, 1995

The Blood Store

After school today,
I had to go to the
Blood store.
When we got there
I told my mommy that
The lab lady already
Took all my blood
Last time,
And now it was
Mommy's turn.
I said, "Ow-ee, ow-ee, ow-ee!"
Even before we went inside.
I was sad
And scared
And wanted Mommy
To hold me.
I wanted her
To pick me up until
It was all through,
Until next time
When I will be
Sad and scared
All over again.

December 20, 1993

My Mommy and Me

Oooowwww . . .
Oooohhhh . . .
My muscles hurt so much . . .
My legs are tired and
My arms are tired and
My head and everything else
Are so, so tired.
Maybe,
Someone needs to get me a
Little boy wheelchair and some
Little boy crutches and some
Little boy ordinary glasses
To help me.
Then my mommy and I
Can crawl around together,
And get each other all better,
Together.

December 3, 1994

91

Easter Drawings

Last spring,
At Easter time,
My friend at school
Drew a picture
Of a little boy
Without any legs.
He only had skin,
And he couldn't walk.
He had to hop around
On his bottom
And his skin.
I think that
Would hurt a little boy.
So, last spring,
At Easter time,
I drew a picture
Of a wheelchair.
Now the little boy
With no legs
Can zoom around,
Without hurting.

August 4, 1994

Jill and Simba

Oh bother!
My stuffed animal,
Baby Simba,
Has diabetes.
He can't eat any sugar,
Or any candy,
Or any cream puffs,
Ever again.
Maybe he got too near Jill
At my mommy's work
And caught them from her.
Jill has diabetes.
Jill and Simba are the same.
Except that Jill's diabetes
Will never go away,
And Baby Simba's diabetes
Will be gone in two days
Because they are
Only make-believe.
I wish I could make Jill's be
Only make-believe,
So she could eat sugar
And candy and cream puffs
And not die.

February 25, 1995

Distant Loss

Dear God,
Please bless Sandy's grandmother
Who died this morning.
Please help her to
Rise into Heaven,
To be with You forever.
Please help her to know
What Heaven is all about,
And to be with
Jamie, and Katie and Stevie,
And all the other good people
Who have died into Heaven.
Please help Sandy
To not miss her too much,
And to feel her spirit
In her heart now.
And I ask this of You,
Our God,
Amen.

April 21, 1995

If for Today . . .

If my brother, Jamie,
Was alive today . . .
He would be eleven years old
And play and read with me.
If my brother, Jamie,
Was alive today . . .
He would help me in hard times
And be my best friend.
If my brother, Jamie,
Was alive today . . .
He would like spending time
With our mommy, just like me.
If my brother, Jamie,
Was alive today . . .
I would hug him
And spend time with him, and
I would do nice things for him
And protect him, and
I would spend time with him
Together, with our mommy, and
I would celebrate life, thanking
God for such a special gift
. . . If my brother, Jamie,
Was alive today.

November 5, 2000

93

Stormy Heartsongs

Examination of Faith (I)

Dear God,
Tonight's prayer is a very
Special and important prayer.
I know that You are good, God,
I know You're great and powerful.
I know that You made everything,
And in the end, all good things
Come back to You, God.
I know You can make miracles happen.
So, I want to tell You about a
Special and important miracle
That I am praying for You to do now.
Margie is growing a baby
Inside of her, like Mary grew Jesus.
But the baby is very little,
And might be very sick.
I am praying that You watch
Over this baby, God,
And that You make a miracle
So that this baby gets stronger
And stronger and stronger so
It can grow and be born.
Please, God, please do this miracle.
I don't want Margie to cry,
Or her husband or her two little girls.
And if their little baby dies,
They will all cry, and me, too.
I even know that You will cry, God,
So of this I ask You, oh Lord.
Amen.

March 22, 1996

94

Examination of Faith (III)

Dear God,
Today is the first day I saw Margie
Since the baby growing in her died.
I told her I was sorry and sad for her.
I told her we all prayed for her and
Her family and the little baby.
I know Margie is sad, even though
She never got to see or touch or
Hold her little baby.
I know that because today is
My brother Stevie's "Angel Day."
It's the day he died except
It was a lot of years ago.
I never saw him, or touched him.
I never knew him, but he was mine.
He was my brother.
He still is my brother, but he is in Heaven.
And even though I never got
To know Stevie,
It still makes me so sad
To not have him here with me.
He is happy in Heaven,
With my other brother, Jamie,
And with my sister, Katie,
And now, with Margie's little baby.
Please take care of Margie, God,
And the baby's sisters and daddy, too.
I know they are sad that their baby died.
Please help them to be happy
Until they finally meet their
Baby in Heaven.

March 24, 1996

Planning Ahead

Mommy,
When I die and you bury me into my box,
You must send with me
My Mr. Bunny, and Jamie's other Mr. Bear,
And also some of Jamie's
Other stuffed animals and toys.
I will take them down and up
Into Heaven with me.
Jamie will be so excited to see me,
And he will be so happy to see
His old toys and other Mr. Bear again.
Then, we can play and play and pray.
And then when you die,
Sandy can send some special things
For you and for me,
And for Jamie, and Katie and Stevie.
And when Sandy dies,
Hedder or Nell or
Someone like that
Can send special things for us
In her box.
And when they all die,
Well, maybe they can
Die holding on to some special things
So that they can bring them
All into Heaven.
And then,
We'll all be together again!
And sometimes if we want
We can play with our special things.
And all the times we can be together,
And never be apart again.

January 9, 1996

Another Asthma Spell

My nose is scratchy and
My voice is funny, like
A teenager-boy who is
Changing to a man-voice.
My cough is like soda
Snipping at you when
You open it, but a
Little bit louder and it's
Again and again and again.
My breathing is wheezing and
My lungs are groaning and
My body is moaning . . .
And it's all because I am
Having another asthma spell.
I hope that my nose and voice
Stop scratching and changing.
I hope that my cough
Stops the soda-snipping.
I hope that my breathing and
My lungs and my body all stop
Wheezing and groaning
And wheezing and moaning . . .
I want to feel all better, and
Not be having
Another asthma spell.

October 21, 1996

Sour Milk Muscles

Aching and burning
And aching and sore . . .
Sour milk muscles are
Hurting once more . . .
Tired and aching
And aching and tight . . .
Sour milk muscles
Are burning tonight . . .
Like too much of milk
Makes your stomach turn sick,
Like too much of stress
Makes your old ulcer tick,
Like too much of acid
Makes everything pain,
These sour milk muscles
Will drive me insane . . .
Aching and burning
And aching and sore . . .
Sour milk muscles are
Hurting once more . . .
Tired and aching
And aching and tight . . .
My sour milk muscles
Have me crying tonight . . .

November 17, 1999

98

Stormy Heartsongs

Preschool Peer Pressure

Do you know why I'm crying?
I'm crying because
I can't do things like
All the other kids outside.
I'm crying because
I can't rollerblade and
I can't ride a bike and
I can't catch a ball and
I can't run so fast and
I keep falling down.
I get scared when I try
To do all those things
Because I fall.
I try not to fall over,
But I always still do.
I am not smart.
Even at Hapkido,
I fall and wiggle-waggle.
I punch down and
I don't point my heel to the mirror.
I am not smart.
If I was smart,
I could think and focus
About all those things
And then do them.
And then the kids would say,
"Hey Mattie! You want to
Come out and play with us?"
They wouldn't just leave me
Because I can't do it.

And then they wouldn't say
"Hey Mattie! How come
You can't do this? It's easy?"
Reading doesn't make me smart.
Manners don't make me smart.
Spelling and numbers
Don't make me smart.
Smart is thinking about something
And doing it without waggling
And without falling and crying.
The kids say I'm not smart because
They just don't want
To read and write or
To do indoor games.
I am angry and sad and
I am disappointed at myself.
And that's why I'm crying
Like a wimpy baby,
Because I do things
Like a wimpy baby.
Maybe I'll say
I can't read anymore, so
I can learn to do
All of those other things.
I need Mr. Bunny
To wipe away my tears.
I need a hug, and
I need a kiss.

February 9, 1995

99

Dear God,

I've been having these dreams,
That make me think that it is real,
And that it will really happen.
Like about a monster taking me away from
Home without anything to take with me and
I never see my mother again.
Dear God,
Please help me have some special medicine
That will get rid of all these nightmares
About going away, and leaving, and dying.
Dear God,
I will thank You for the special medicine,
Even if it's invisible medicine that is
Inside of all the healthy food I eat every day,
Or inside of all the meditation I do every day.
Dear God,
I send You big hugs and big kisses, and
You will send me the invisible medicine
To cure this scariness and
To get over these feelings and nightmares.
Please put it into all of the food that I eat
So they won't come ever again,
Even while I am still getting better.
I need to get rid of this tiredness in my heart.
Amen.

August 10, 1996

Stormy Heartsongs

Treading Time

For so very long,
A hurdle was in front of me.
I couldn't move forward.
I couldn't jump over it.
I couldn't go around it.
It was there, and
I couldn't get on with things,
But I couldn't stop running.
And I didn't want
To go backward.
But I have a great advocate.
She is the best.
She has influence.
She is strong.
She has some power.
She moved the hurdle.
She couldn't take it away,
But she moved it.

Now, I am still running,
But the hurdle is beside me.
It is still there,
But it is not blocking my way.
It is not behind me, and
It may get moved
In front again,
Or I might get so very tired of
Running away next to it and
It will win to the front.
But for now,
It is not right in front of me.
I will run even faster, and
My advocate will get
Even stronger.
And some day,
I will leave that hurdle
In my dust.

October 27, 1998

Life Bible Story

The story of Exodus—
When Moses and
Aaron fought
The Egyptian Pharaoh
With God's powers to
Free the Hebrew slaves—
Is very much like my own life.
When I was born,
Many people were not sure
That I would live.
Moses almost perished
From the evil of the ruler.
I almost perished
From the danger of disease.
But, under good care,
I lived, just like Moses.
I have had life experiences
That were mean and hurtful,
Just like the Pharaoh hurt
Moses' people, the Hebrews.

But with the help of God
And many good,
Helpful friends,
I was able to find
Freedom and sanctuary.
Like the pilgrimage of Moses,
It is taking a long time
To find the
"Promised land" of my life.
The journey is filled with
Unknowns and ongoing fear,
And I am not sure when
I might make it to real safety.
But, I feel that
Events in my life
Are similar to
That of Moses' life,
And so, God will be with me
As I search faithfully for,
And find, a better future.

April 22, 2000

Vultures

Nature takes its course,
And an animal dies.
Soon, it shall turn to dust,
But not yet,
For even though its death is sad,
It helps other animals live
So that they do not starve.
Swarms of flies come
To take their share,
Followed by a pack of hyenas,
All of them waiting
To have their turn.
Then, from above,
A single vulture
Spots the carcass, and
Calls its fellow buzzards to join.
First, only one vulture appears,
Then another,
And another, and another,
Until an army of black birds
Makes a cloud in the sky.
Then, they swiftly swoop
Down,
    Down,
        Down,

Around,
    And around,
        And around,
Forming a giant,
Cawing tornado
To announce the great feast.
Then, they disappear
To the ground,
To finish up the remains
Of the dead animal.
When done, they swiftly swoop
Back to their tree branches,
Waiting . . .
    Waiting . . .
        Waiting . . .
Waiting for the next feast to fall
To the ground under them.
Although it is sad
That the animal died,
And sad to see
The vultures eat it,
It is nature.
All living things die,
And the vultures must
Clean it up by eating it,
It always has and
It always will happen, because
It is nature, taking its course.

April 17, 2000

Life-Storm

The wind marches in,
A thousand man army
Howling,
Stiff,
Blowing straight, and
Twisting through
Everything in its path.
Who knows where
It comes from . . .
Or why?
Who knows where
It is going to . .
Or what it shall do
Next?
It leaves
Destruction,
Devastation,
Even death,
Everywhere
It attacks.
So much like
The life
Of some people,
Too many people,
Angry, hurting people . . .
Marching around,
Blowing around,
Dying and lost,
In raging lives.

January 11, 2000

Unfinished

Seeping silently in the night
Dark before the sun's first light
The deuce of death not yet in sight
Life awaiting dawn . . .
Fires, fires, fires fell
The horror, a sight straight from hell
Why fire attacks, it will never tell
Death before the dawn . . .
Life cries out for help from friends
Will the hatred ever end?
The screams of frightened souls will send
Desperate prayer to survive 'til dawn . . .
The fires, the fires, slowly die down
Ending their horrendous sound
Secure-like feeling will soon come 'round
Arriving with the dawn . . .
From fire and fear
Such presence so near
To peace of a dove
Some future, some year
And yet we still ponder
The next day, what next . . .
Live in fear or choose fight
Live in fear or choose might
Live in fear or choose flight
Why choose any such sight
For not one is right
If we choose to count
On this and each night . . .
To wake with another dawn.

March 24, 2003

104

What Is Good?

Isn't it so sad
That people fight each other?
And sometimes,
People kill each other.
Even good people
Kill other people.
That is so, so, so
Terrible and horrible.
Like in Bosnia . . .
The United States soldiers
Have to go there so that
The bad guy soldiers don't
Kill the people there anymore.
And that means
That a good soldier might
Have to kill a bad soldier,
Even if he or she does
Not want to kill anyone at all.
And I know that
The good soldier is good,
But how can anyone
Still be good when
They have killed someone else?
I just don't understand . . .
And all that fighting
In Bosnia started because
Some people didn't like
The way some of the other
People prayed, or talked,
Or played, or looked.

It's just so, so, so sad.
I really don't think this is what
God wanted for His people,
Or for His earth.
I really don't think this is why
God made us
And gave us all of our gifts.
I really don't think we are
Listening to God in our hearts.
And worst of all,
I really don't think God
Is very happy at all
With all of this fighting
And killing and hating.
I'm sorry, God.
I'm so, so, so sorry . . .
I wish all of the soldiers
Could and would
Listen to the children,
Because *we know* that
Fighting is wrong.
But I think that the grown-ups
Sometimes forget
What is good and
What is right . . .
For people, and
For Earth, and
For God.

January 2, 1996

105

The Rules of War

The rules of war have changed.
We've moved
From battlefields to backyards,
From arrows to anthrax,
From ninjas to nuclear weapons,
From swords to seron gas.
We used to
Fight for a just cause.
Now we
Fight, just because.
We used to win
Hand-to-hand,
Face-to-face.
Now we merely hear of
Children in mass graves
Mingled with the grown-ups
Who were protecting them
And their interests.
We are destroying everything
That we claim to be fighting for.
We can not win
Today's war with bombs.
We must resolve
Our issues with words.
The rules of war have changed.
How can we choose to continue
Playing this deadly
And impersonal game of loss?

January 20, 2003

106

Tele Vision

I kept my eyes
Open to the future.
Open and bright,
Never clouded with
Remnants of things
That just weren't right.
But 9/11 blew up
So very much dust
That we had to
Keep our eyes
Closed to the pain.
Closed and tight,
Ever shrouded with
Remains of those
Who just weren't the fight.

Now, together, let us
Close our eyes gently and
Bow our heads reverently,
Prayers on our lips,
Goodwill on our fingertips
Touching the world with
A meek and humble
Gesture of humanity.
And perhaps,
We can one day,
Open our eyes
To a gentle tomorrow.
We will keep our eyes
Open to the future.
Open and bright,
Never clouded or dusted with
Remnants of things or
Remains of those that
Just weren't right for a fight.

July 17, 2002

107

Stormy Heartsongs

Prayer for the Earth, and People

Dear God,
Please help us, God!
We must stop the anger!
We must stop the violence!
We must stop it in people,
In families, in countries, in earth!
People are sad when they are angry.
Families are sad when they are angry.
Countries have war when they are angry.
And when there is war,
There is sadness, and violence,
And the people die,
And the families die,
And the countries die,
And even the earth will die.
Nine is such a good number
For planets in our universe.
It would be a shame to only have eight
Planets if this one disappears from people.
And because Earth is the only planet
That's not too hot and not too cold and
That has the right air and water for life,
Well, it would be even more of a shame,
Because we'd all disappear with the planet.
Please, help us, God.
I want my planet.
I want my family.
I want my life.
Amen.

May 5, 1996

Stormy Heartsongs

Playful Heartsongs

I will be a whenwolf with the sun, and
A whichwolf with the almost moons, and
A whywolf with the invisible moon.
But always watch out, and beware, because
I am a werewolf for any moon . . .

Excerpt from "Beware, of the Ever-Wolf" by Mattie J.T. Stepanek,
in *Journey Through Heartsongs* (Hyperion/VSP, 2002)

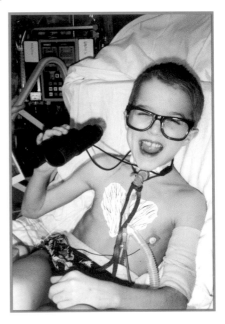

PREVIOUS PAGE: A big smile from Mattie, summer 1997

TOP: Mattie swinging during a day in the mountains, summer 1998

BOTTOM LEFT: Mattie cooling off on a hot summer day, summer 1998

BOTTOM RIGHT: Mattie as Austin Powers . . . "yeah, baby!" summer 2001

An inarticulate doctor is following Oprah Winfrey [in offering these Tributes today]. Mattie got the last laugh. . . .

Medical failure with Mattie was inevitable. We were never going to win. Yet his spirit and enthusiasm made it oh-so-easy to try. He had adult thoughts, but he was a child. And that was, in large part, his magic.

In 2001, before his notoriety, [we worked to] help him with three wishes. And the magic of his soul just brought so many people at Children's National Medical Center together to help him meet those wishes. He wanted to talk peace with Jimmy Carter. He wanted to spread his message [of hope] on The Oprah Winfrey Show. And, he wanted to publish his poetry. Before anyone knew of him, this was his vision. And yet, the strength and spirit of this young person was just so . . . different, interesting, that he brought people together to help him with that vision.

He had adult thoughts, but he was a child. Mattie was a world-class prankster. He really did put apple juice in the urine cup and drink it in front of a doctor. He really did watch Ferris Bueller's Day Off just to get some inspiration. He really did make liberal use of his fart machine. His remote-control whoopee cushion is with him now, as is his Grey Hero, the stuffed animal wolf that was always touching him, as it is now. He had adult thoughts, but he was a child.

A single thought that we will try to remember when we think of Mattie is the line from the front of your booklet, "Always remember to play after every storm." Thank you.

—Dr. Murray Pollack
(Division Chief, Critical Care Medicine,
Children's National Medical Center, Washington, D.C.)

Tribute by Dr. Murray Pollack during the funeral of Mattie J.T. Stepanek on June 28, 2004, Wheaton, Maryland

Playful Heartsongs

*C*onsidering all the challenges, all the losses, all the unknowns, all the ongoing emotional and physical pain that was part of Mattie's entire life, it is amazing that he was such an optimistic, inspiring, confident, and genuinely happy human being. When he was in kindergarten, a television reporter was interviewing him about his first poetry book, *Heartsongs,* which he had submitted for a countywide contest in the public school system. I was sitting in the next room, and overheard her ask my five-year-old child, "So, Mattie, do you have a philosophy for your life?"

Chuckling to myself, I wondered why an adult would even think that such a young child would know what the word "philosophy" meant, much less have contemplated a guiding principle for his personal life. To my astonishment, Mattie answered her without hesitation, "Oh, yes, ma'am. My life philosophy is 'always remember to play after every storm.'" And he proceeded to explain to her what he meant by the various "storms" we encounter in life, and the important matter of "playing" as a source of celebration, rejuvenation, and appreciation.

Mattie recognized and understood at a very early age that sadness, even anguish, can be balanced into something bearable, even acceptable and meaningful, if we choose to journey through life with a hopeful attitude. Although he had moments with tears, he was also able to find reason and opportunity to laugh with other children and with adults in the truly best of times, and in the truly worst of times. Even when he had to live for months at a time in the traumatic environment of the Pediatric Intensive Care Unit, Mattie created great pleasure for professionals, families, other patients, and himself through conversation, playful interactions, and practical jokes.

While he enjoyed classic board and card games, Mattie also loved to play imaginatively, inventing characters for an illustrative story or involving established characters for some new lesson in life. Riding in the van, waiting in a long line, whether summer camp or a stay in the hospital was at hand, we created word games and mind games and any other games possible for the sake of smiling together, or at least for the sake of focusing on something other than whatever storm might be forming.

This chapter, Playful Heartsongs, is filled with selections from Mattie's lighter experiences and expressions. The reader meets a child who plays with ideas and words while creating poetry that dances through seasons and finds solace in sorrow. In reading these passages, we realize how one child was able to reflect on a personal life philosophy and find strength and resiliency for himself, for others, and for the world.

112

Playful Heartsongs

On Being Content

Sometimes,
I wish I was a cow,
Grazing on a hillside and
Lowing with my friends and
Kneeling in the soft grass to
Protect me from tears of rain . . .
But then I remember,
Sometimes, cows become hamburger.
Sometimes,
I wish I had a flat tongue,
Like that of a dog
Lapping water by the scoop and
Licking ice cream by the gallon and
Looking so very unique and cool . . .
But then I remember,
Sometimes, girls don't like dog kisses.
Sometimes,
I wish I was a someone,
Or an anyone other than
The me that I am, who
Can not keep up and who
May not stay in but who
Will not give in, or up . . .
But then I remember,
Sometimes, that
I am uniquely cool and
I kneel in the protection of God,
Who created me to be,
Just who and as I am.

May 16, 2002

Geography Lesson

I've been to Maryland—
That's where I live.
And I've been to Florida—
That's where
Grandaddy lived.
I've been to North Carolina—
That's where
Mommy took me
When she went
On her business trip.
And I've even
Been to Canada—
That's where
Mommy took me
When she and Sandy
Went on her
'Nother business trip.
But I haven't been to France.
And, I'm not sure
If I want to go there.
My cousin, David,
Went to France—
And he told me that
That's where
The "Awful Tower" lives.

July 1, 1994

Oh Bother!

Oh bother!
Mattie has turned
Into a hiccup!
Watch . . .
Hiccup!
Hiccup!
Hiccup!
Now,
He will go
Into other people,
And they will
Get the hiccups, too!
He will go
Into their tummies.
And after
Twenty-five days,
The hiccups
Will go away,
All by themselves.
And Mattie will crawl
Out of their mouths.
Whew!
Just hope
Mattie doesn't turn
Into a hiccup again!

August 28, 1994

114

Good Rain Sense

When the clouds are all
Bunched up and gray . . .
When you hear a
Split-splat begin to
Tip-tap against a
Leaf, or the ground . . .
When the thick smell
That comes before a
Storm heavies the air . . .
When you feel like
Everything around
Hurries you to
Get inside quickly . . .
It's time to be like
Christopher Robin and say:
"Tut-tut! It looks like rain!"

September 22, 1998

Snow Flurry Dance

The first snow flurry of the year!
It's happened today,
The snow flurry is here!
Snow flurries
Make me so happy!
Cars wear white caps, and
Houses wear white blankets.
Plants wear white lace
On their leaves, and
Children wear big smiles and
Dance in the snow flurries
Singing "thank you" and
"Hooray!" for the white magic
They catch on their tongues!
The first snow flurry of the year!
Seasons are changing, and
Cold weather is coming, and
Plants get to sleep and rest, and
People get to see
The beautiful snows . . .
And children get to grow into
Another season and
Be so happy!

November 14, 1996

115

Morning Routine

By the time
Auntie Flora dies,
She'll have gone
To every
Dunkin' Donuts
In Maryland;
Or, perhaps, to
One, two, or three
Different ones
At least
Three hundred times.

February 11, 2000

Blah . . .

Rainy Sundays
Are fuzzy days,
Stuck between
The end
Of the past week,
And the start
Of a new one.

October 9, 1999

Aaaaahh . . .

A warm bath,
A gentle foot massage,
A fuzzy blanket . . .
Oh, how wonderful
To have these
Soothing gifts of life.

November 9, 1999

My Mother . . .

A very unique personality.
Stands out from the rest.
My mother . . .
Writer of Gracenotes.
Lover of chocolate.
Observer of news.
Believer in the Clean Dish Fairy.
My mother . . .
Flexible in activities.
Free time on the computer.
Drinker of coffee and afternoon tea.
My mother . . .
Totally fun and zany.
A Dweeb—"Dweebcy."
But then again,
I am little "Dweebky."
Proud, proud, proud to be a Dweeb.
My mother . . .
Caring.
Gentle.
Loving.
My mother . . .
My greatest teacher in life.
About life.
For life.
I love you, my mother.
Your ways shape
My being and future.
Your uniqueness will live forever
As I pass your
Lessons of the heart
On to my children.

February 22, 2000

Metaphor Lesson (III)

A mother is
A gentle lioness
Trying to defend her cubs,
Sometimes more than she can.

Metaphor Lesson (VII)

A pesky dog
Is a pile of homework,
Always there,
Gnawing for attention.

Metaphor Lesson (IV)

When one is sad,
A friend is
A familiar
Security blanket.

Metaphor Lesson (XI)

A constantly buzzing fly
Is a school day
That drags on, then
Goes into overtime.

Metaphor Lesson (V)

Too often,
The doctor is
A mosquito
Prepared to bite.

Metaphor Lesson (XIV)

Often, my vivid imagination
Is a rapidly spreading fire,
Consuming page after page
Of my personal journal.

March 30, 2000

Believing

You believe in me,
So I believe in me.
Because I believe in me,
I can believe in others,
And in the
Goodness of the world.

July 9, 2003

Splash-Adventure

Splash, splash, I'm taking a bath,
Oh, how much fun I always have,
When I'm splashing and taking a bath.
But now it's time
To pull up the plug,
It's time for me to get
Out of the tub,
So I pull up the plug
To get out of the tub, and . . .
Oh, bother! Oh, dear!
What's happening now?
My toe,
It's caught in the drain!
I'm going out with the water,
Out down in the drain.
My toe and my leg and
My very whole me is
Going, going, going down the drain!
Into the old-water pipes
Under the house, under the street,
Into the river, into the sea.
I wonder if Mommy knows
What's happened to me?
Oh look, there's a cloud and it's over the sea,
And now I'm going up into the clouds
With all of this ocean water vanished from the sea.
Hey, the cloud is going back over the land,
And it's raining and raining all over the land.
I come down with the water and
Into the river, and into the new-water pipes
Under the street, under the house.
And my mommy is sad, sad, sad . . .

Playful Heartsongs

"Oh, where is my baby?
Oh, where can he be?"
And she will cry and cry and cry.
And then Mommy will
Be thirsty from all that crying.
And Mommy will go to the sink
And she'll turn on the water
To fill up a glass . . .
And all of a sudden . . .
What have we here?
A toe!
A knee!
A tummy!
A hand!
A head!
A whole little me!!!
"Gosh, Mom, did you miss me?
I went out of the drain and
Into the pipes and the sea and the clouds
And then all the way back home!"
She'll hug me and say,
"I'm so glad you are back,
But my, look how dirty you are!"
And I will go upstairs
To take a bath . . .
And I wonder what will happen next?!

January 20, 1995

121

Playful Heartsongs

Cat-Tale

Meow! Meow!
Meow! Meow!
I am a little kittycat.
My name is Krispie Kittycat.
See? I have hand-paws,
And I have feet-paws.
I am hungry . . .
Please give me some cat food.
I am lonely . . .
Please scratch me
Behind my ears.
Meow! Meow!
That's nice love.
I will sit in your lap,
And you can
Pet me some more.
Meow! Meow!
Meow! Meow!
Please sing me a song
About kittycats.
The one with the
Kittens and mittens.
I will be very gentle,
And I will not scratch you . . .
But just don't touch my tail.

September 30, 1993

Dragon-song

If a dragon sang a song,
What would the
Dragon-song sound like?
Greedy fire-drake dragons
Sing a song of self-pride . . .
Of personal treasure and
Victories of gluttony,
To boast and strike
Fear and jealousy in all.
Lonely loch-ness dragons
Sing a song of solitude . . .
Of isolated existence and
Needs of friendly love,
To express feelings and
Cry out for company.
Mythical fairy-tale dragons
Sing a song of clandestine ends . . .
Of revealing to chosen ones,
Believers who make the choice
To understand the nature,
The sense, the imagination
. . . Of a Dragon-song.

September 18, 2001

122

The Pirate Song

Shiver my temper,
Shiver my soul,
W-O-E . . .
     W-O-E . . .
          W-O-E!
Shiver my temper,
Shiver my soul,
Woe, ho, hum,
And a bucket of rum!
I am a pirate
So nasty and mean,
I never take a bath
And my teeth are all green.
I snarl and I snortle
And I gurgle my juice,
My clothes are all dirty
And my socks are too loose!
     Shiver my temper,
     Shiver my soul,
     W-O-E . . .
          W-O-E . . .
               W-O-E!
     Shiver my temper,
     Shiver my soul,
     Woe, ho, hum,
     And a bucket of rum!
I've sailed the high seas
And a backyard pool,
I've buried my treasure
'Cause I am no fool.
I've hidden the maps
In a secret-somewhere,
And if you try to find them
You'd better beware!

Shiver my temper,
Shiver my soul,
W-O-E . . .
     W-O-E . . .
          W-O-E!
Shiver my temper,
Shiver my soul,
Woe, ho, hum,
And a bucket of rum!
Don't try to dig
In the sand or the night,
Or you might just shake
From a terrible fright.
'Cause even if my ghost
Is a skinless dust of bone,
I'll be guarding my treasure
With a plundering moan!
     Shiver my temper,
     Shiver my soul,
     W-O-E . . .
          W-O-E . . .
               W-O-E!
     Shiver my temper,
     Shiver my soul,
     Woe, ho, hum,
     And a bucket of rum!

July 4, 1998

123

Cowboy Facts

Cowboys love their horses.
Cowboys keep food with them.
Bandits are enemies of cowboys.
Wise cowboys like American Indians.
Cowboys always have a name for their horse.
Cowboys sometimes wear hats of straw.
Cowboys wear big, tough, leather boots.
Cowboys often live on frontiers or
Ranches near the desert.
Singing under the stars around the
Campfire is a favorite for cowboys.
Some cowboys still sleep with
Their teddy bears.

June 18, 1998

Porcelain Haiku

I am not a king.
I don't own a castle. But
I sit on a throne.

March 24, 2000

Dear Mr. Lincoln

I met a man
From the past, and
I told him about
Our today.
He told me about
His yesterday, and
Together,
We discovered
All the spaces and
All the stories
That grew in between.

May 30, 2002

124

The Importance of Teddy Bears

Teddy bears are very important to life.
Even if they look a lot like the same,
No two teddy bears are exactly alike.
They are different . . . just like people.
Some have black fur, brown faces, and a red tie, and
Some have white fur, pluffy bodies, and no clothes.
Some have eyes you can hardly see behind the fur, and
Some have big blue or black or brown eyes that shine.
Some have little or big tails or paws or noses, and
Some have a heart on their chest that says "I love you."
Some have voices that sound when you squeeze a paw, and
Some have very quiet voices that you can only hear in your mind,
But all teddy bears speak to you when you need them, and
When you are ready to listen to the lesson they will share.
Teddy bears love their people, and people love their teddy bears.
Teddy bears are warm and soft and cuddly.
They will snuggle up with you when you sleep,
They will go with you to the doctors, and when you die,
They will even go with you through the earth into Heaven.
Without a fuzzy little buddy, people will get very sad and lonely.
If everyone had a teddy bear,
The world could be a more cuddly and peaceful place, and
People would not be lonely or sad, or angry about whatever.
The whole world needs a teddy bear, and
That's why teddy bears are so important to life.

June 1, 1997

Problems, Problems, Problems

Problems are like pimples,
Always out of place . . .
And just like many other zits,
They're always in your face!

Problems are like crickets,
Annoying as can be . . .
And if you don't just deal with them,
They'll bark you up a tree!

Problems are like bullies,
Bugging you to death . . .
But one sure way to lure them gone,
Is let them smell your breath!

Problems are like schoolwork,
Always in your way . . .
And if you don't get rid of them,
They'll ruin every day!

Problems, problems, problems,
Forever causing strife . . .
But don't let problems get you down,
Or you'll miss out on life!

October 24, 2000

Easy Transportation

When I have body pains,
It is very uncomfortable
To move,
To shift positions, and
To get from here to there.
When I have body pains,
I wish that I had a special vehicle
To take me around the house.
Not my wheelchair, but a craft
That hovers above the ground, and
Responds to an
Oral command system.
There would be no effort or bumps.
It would not be so uncomfortable
To move,
To shift positions, and
To get from here to there.
"Seat up slowly, please."
"More cushion below my knees."
"Take me to my bedroom, please."
Aaahhh . . .
That is what I need
When I have body pains.
That is what my mom needs, too.
I will let her use my
Easy Transportation Device
Whenever she has body pains.
Then she will not hurt as much,
And I will feel better, too.

November 6, 2000

Playful Heartsongs

Morning Shoes

Listen . . .
Listen carefully to the people
When they are walking to work,
Or to school, or to play,
Or even to wherever,
And the shoes can tell you what
Kind of breakfast cereal their people eat.
The ladies hurrying in pointy high-heels eat
      Coco-coco-coco-poppin'
      Coco-coco-coco-poppin' . . .
The men with boots and heavy steps eat
      Crunchabooma-crunchabooma
      Crunchabooma-crunchabooma . . .
The teenagers who forget to tie their sneakers eat
      Sugar-chewy-munchy-boomy
      Sugar-chewy-munchy-boomy . . .
The children in sandals and velcro shoes eat
      Twinkle-crinkle-marshmallow-sprinkle,
      Twinkle-crinkle-marshmallow-sprinkle . . .
And the old man in his bedroom slippers at the bus stop eats
      Snap-crackle-rustle-pop,
      Snap-crackle-rustle-pop . . .
But the babies in their strollers with little soft shoes
That have no dirt marks on the bottoms of them
Don't make any noise at all . . .
That's because they eat oatmeal,
And listen to hear what the grown-ups eat
So they know what to ask for when they get older.

August 14, 1995

The Sunday Drive

Every Sunday,
We keep Holy the Sabbath,
Just like God asked us to do
In His Ten Commandments.
Every Sunday,
We drive to church and
We say prayers and
We sing songs and
We be together with all
Of our Church-Friends.
And every Sunday,
We see animals while we
Are driving down the
Twisty-turny-windy road . . .
Except that none of the
Animals were there today!
Where, oh where could they be?
I know! This Sunday,
The animals went to
Animal-Church to pray like us.
The horses say "Neigh-men!"
The sheep say "Baaaaa-men!"
The cows say "A-moo!"
The ducks say "Quack-men!"
Even the wind in the trees and
The tall blowing grass say
"Swoosh-men!"
God hears them all together
With the people who are saying
"Amen—I believe!" and
"Alleluia—Praise the Lord!"
Wow!
What a Whole-Holy-Sabbath!

February 25, 1995

Headstones

I saw Heaven again.
It was not the same Heaven
That Jamie died into.
It was a different Heaven,
But all the Heavens come together,
And all the people who died
Can go all over to the
Different Heaven-Cemeteries.
And in this Heaven,
There were twenty-five things
For Jamie to play
Hide-and-seek behind.
Twenty-five is a number
For a lot of money,
Or a lot of birthdays,
Or a lot of things to hide behind.
But Jamie is so special,
That he needs all of those
Things to play with.
I played hide-and-seek with Jamie
At his Heaven-Cemetery.
Maybe someday,
I can come to this Heaven-Cemetery
And play with him here!

July 3, 1994

128

Hugging-Jamie

We used to
Hug Jamie
When we lived
At our Older-House,
Before he died.
I remember doing that.
I remember I liked to
Hug Jamie.
I love Jamie.
Now we live
At our New-House.
Jamie's
Muscles-and-bones died.
Sometimes,
I think about Jamie,
And I think about
Hugging Jamie.
Sometimes,
I hug invisible Jamie.
I share my
Toys with him.
I say,
"Here, Jamie,
Here's a toy for you!"
And Jamie smiles his
Angel-Smile.
Today I say,
"Here, Jamie,
Have some of my food!"

And Jamie-Angel smiles
And he eats food
From his Living-Brother.
Then,
Very gently,
Just like before Jamie died,
I pat him and pat him
And pat him.
Do you know
What happens next?
Jamie burps an Angel-Burp!
An invisible Angel-Burp
From my invisible
Angel-Brother.
That is very funny, isn't it!?!
Funny things
Make me happy,
But I would be even happier
If I could have my
Real-Brother
Back from Heaven,
So I could really
Pat him and hug him and
Hold him and love him and
See him and be with him and
Feel his muscles-and-bones
Instead of just his Spirit.

June 12, 1994

129

Playful Heartsongs

Star-Light and Angel-Rides

A star with a tail on it is an Angel-Ride!
Angels can be in the stars you know.
Sometimes Jamie is in the stars,
And if he sees a bright tail-star,
He can ride across the sky
And across the world
With the light of the stars.
He can ride across the Heavens
With the Light of the Stars,
Which is the Light of the World,
Which is our Creator,
Who lights our way in life.

March 7, 1996

Sacred Heartsongs

Just look out into the sunrise,
Then jump into your own heart,
Float into the air like in a dream,
And pray with love and praise and thank-yous
For your life, for your spirit, for your sunrise . . .
And for being a part of this heavenly crystal ball!

Excerpt from "Crystal Celebration" by Mattie J.T. Stepanek,
in *Journey Through Heartsongs* (Hyperion/VSP, 2002)

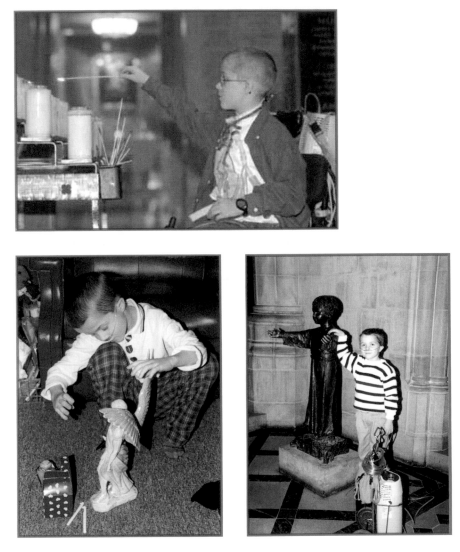

PREVIOUS PAGE: Mattie praying at the National Cathedral, winter 1996

TOP: Mattie lighting candles in the National Shrine of the Immaculate Conception, winter 2003

BOTTOM LEFT: Mattie admiring an angel statue, spring 1998

BOTTOM RIGHT: Mattie studies the statues at the National Cathedral, winter 1996

At Most Holy Rosary, our parish where Mattie and his mom belonged, Mattie participated in the celebration of the sacred mysteries. He was a [Minister of the Word] reader, [he helped teach CCD], and he also was a choir member, as was his mother, Jeni. . . . Mattie Stepanek . . . a great gift, who grew up in our parish and who participated with us and who loved us and who gave us such a wonderful example of what it means to be a believer. So he not only accomplished great things, literary things—writing poetry and accounts of his life and all those things he was involved in—but he gave us a great example of embracing the cross. On our baptism day, we are signed with the cross of Jesus Christ. We have Jesus' words that "if you will follow me, you must take up your cross each day and come after me."

So what does it mean to take up the cross? Well it's more than just words. It means that we have to make the sacrifices that come our way, and certainly Mattie had many sacrifices. His whole life long he suffered. We were all very impressed, especially when he had the oxygen tanks. Every time people remember Mattie at our church, they remember when he had those tanks and just darted around from one place to another, very nimbly so. Nothing could slow Mattie down or thwart him. He always remembered his siblings, Jamie, Katie, and Stevie, though he's gone now to be with them, and celebrate with them in God's presence. For the great gift that God makes us, His children, and He makes us so like unto His Son, Jesus Christ, that He invites us to share in the sacrifice of Jesus . . .

—Reverend Father Isidore Dixon
(Pastor, Most Holy Rosary Parish, Rosaryville, Maryland)

Excerpts from homily by Fr. Isidore Dixon during funeral mass of Mattie J.T. Stepanek, June 28, 2004, Wheaton, Maryland

133

Sacred Heartsongs

Religion and spirituality were viewed by Mattie as two very different, though related and important, concepts. Mattie understood religion to be a structural framework, "filled with beliefs and practices and rituals that give shape and support to how we celebrate the joys and cope with the sufferings of life." He considered spirituality to be something more personal, "related to a sense of purpose and being that transcends our mortal understanding of time and space." The integration of religion and spirituality was something Mattie believed could help people make sense of things that are beyond human understanding. But he also believed that such assimilation relied not just on faith, but also on reverence, or respect—for our own choices and for the choices made by others. As long as a religion and spirituality called us to be better, gentler, more peaceful people, with each other and the world, it served a good purpose.

Although he respected all forms of religion, Mattie embraced Catholicism as his creed. Like many Catholics, he was baptized into the Church as an infant. But Mattie had some connection to spirituality that was deeper, more intense, more aware and available and active, than any adult I have ever known. From the time he was able to communicate, Mattie maintained that God spoke to his heart, not with mere words, but with a message that Mattie knew he was to share with the world . . . a message of hope and peace.

At age seven, Mattie took preparatory classes with other children his age, then received First Holy Communion. Only a week later, Cardinal James A. Hickey told me that he had spent time observing and talking with Mattie, and that he believed Mattie had some wisdom, some knowledge and understanding of faith and purpose that was beyond what he sensed in most other people. He asked me if he could offer Mattie the sacrament of Confirmation, something that typically does not occur in the Catholic Church until at least age fourteen. Because of the religious commitment required by this sacrament, I chose to offer Mattie the opportunity to study for a year, learning more about both Catholic doctrine and conventions so that he could make an informed decision whether to be confirmed in this Church. The following spring, Cardinal Hickey was back at our parish confirming a dozen young adults, and eight-year-old Mattie. During the ceremony, the cardinal asks questions of those being confirmed so they can demonstrate their knowledge of the religion. After listening to Mattie's responses, which combined religious doctrine with meaningful interpretations for a life that included joy and suffering, Cardinal Hickey came down from the altar, and kissed Mattie on the head saying, "I have never met any person more ready and understanding of religion, spirituality, this sacrament, than this child here before me today."

In this chapter, Sacred Heartsongs, we are offered Mattie's gift of faith. We witness how one child was inspired to "believe in something bigger and better than the here and now," even without full understanding, and without proof. Through these poems, we see the reflections of a peacemaker, who was blessed with appreciation and respect for the goodness of humanity.

134

Resolution Blessing

Let our breath be gentle wind,
Let our ears be of those who listen,
Let our hearts be not ones
That rage so quickly and
Thus blow dramatically,
And uselessly.
Let our spirits attend and be
Most diligent to the soft
Yet desperate whisper of
Hope and peace for our world.
Let our souls be those
Which watch for the Lord,
Waiting with wonder and want.
Let our eyes be attentive
With interest and respect,
Let our minds be committed
To health and happiness,
Let our hands join
In helpful resolution
To being our best person,
Praying and playing and
Passing through moments
Of pain or memory-
Makers of pleasure
Touching the future, together.

January 1, 2003

Where Is Heaven?

Part of Heaven is
At the cemetery.
Sometimes we go to
Heaven at the cemetery . . .
And sometimes we don't go to
Heaven at the cemetery.
Part of Heaven is
At church.
God is in Heaven,
And He is always on
The walls at church.
And,
Part of Heaven is
In my family
I am in my family,
And so are Jamie,
And Katie and Stevie,
Who are in Heaven.
But they are still
In my family.
So . . .
Part of Heaven is
In my family.

September 28, 1993

Innocent Visions

One time,
I saw Heaven.
And when I saw Heaven,
It was a girl.
And when I looked at the girl,
It looked like a boy.
And that is because
Heaven
Is everyone,
And everything,
And everywhere,
That is good and special.

October 21, 1993

About Praying

When I am very, very sad,
I pray to God to help me
Feel happy and safe again.
When I am very, very angry,
I pray to God to help me
Feel peaceful and nice again.
And when I am very, very happy,
I pray to God, saying,
"Alleluia! Alleluia!
Thank You, God,
Thank You, and Amen!"

August 16, 1995

Love the World

Dear God,
Thank You for all my things,
My toys, my Mr. Bunny, my room.
Thank You for my mother, and
Thank You for my friends.
Thank You for prayer, and
Thank You for my teachers.
Thank You for the world, and
Thank You for opening
The Gates of Heaven.
Thank You for the things we eat,
The things we love, and
The things we do.
Thank You for making nature for us, and
Thank You for making color for us,
Or else I would never have seen
All this mosaic in the world and
I would never have celebrated
So much in each day, and
Learned about the excitement of life.
If there were no world,
It would never be normal.
But it is normal,
Which is amazing,
And I really love my world.
I love You and You love us,
And We love the Heavens
And We love the earth.
Amen.

July 17, 1996

Hush . . .

Whisper earth's name
In a smile, or a sigh,
Whisper earth's name . . .
Await a reply.
Whisper life's name
With a breath of peace,
Whisper life's name . .
Let hope never cease.
Whisper your name
Feel the echo of your voice,
Whisper your name . . .
The silhouette of your choice.
Whisper God's name
In truth's joy, or truth's sorrow,
Whisper God's name . . .
In a prayer for tomorrow.

July 17, 2000

137

Sacred Heartsongs

The Homily

Sometimes,
When I go to Church,
I look at the
Big cross up front and say,
"Hi, Jesus. I came
To pray with you today."
And that makes me happy.
Sometimes,
When I go to Church,
I wave at the
People all around me.
They smile, and sometimes
They wave back at me.
And that makes me happy.
Sometimes,
When I go to Church,
I sit still and
Do good-listening, and
We go to the
School after Church
To have donuts and talk
With our Church-friends.
And that
Makes me happy, too.

But today,
When I went to Church,
Fr. George
Was talking to the people,
And all of a sudden,
I heard him say,
"God is love."
I said, "God is love?"
And Mommy whispered,
"Yes, God is love."
And then I whispered,
"Wow! God is love!"
Jamie is in Heaven with God.
And if God is love,
Jamie is with love!
Heaven really IS
A "wonderful place!"
Then, I thought
Of my brother, Jamie,
Smiling and
Flapping his Angel wings.
And that made me
Very, Very, VERY happy!

May 8, 1994

Angel Words (I)

Mommy,
Do you know what
Jamie
And Katie and Stevie
Say about you in Heaven?
Sometimes,
They say you are
Like the beauty of a rainbow,
As lovely as a flower.
And sometimes,
They follow the star
To Mattie's school
To help watch over me
When you can't be with me.
They say,
"We love you, Mommy.
We will see you again.
One day,
As you will see us,
In Heaven."

January 15, 1995

Prayer for Children

Dear God,
Please help us
Not to judge your miracles,
But to take after
The children of the world,
Innocent and pure in faith.
Let us remember
That the children's
Kingdom of Heaven
Does not mean such is
Merely for the young,
But for those who are
Young at heart and
Innocent in thought and
Pure in the faith of goodness.
For this, we pray,
For the world and
For the children.
Amen.

September 10, 2001

139

On Being

God did not say
"I am who Will."
Nor did God say
"I am who Can," or
"I am who Might."
Rather, God said
"I am who Am."
Let us be like God,
As we were created
To be, then.
Let us not say
"I am someone
Who will change,
Who can do better,
Who might be gentler."
Rather, let us pray
And let us say,
"I am someone
Who is loving,
Who is peaceful,
Who is thankful for
The fact that I am."

June 4, 2002

Proving Faith

I am inclined to
A natural religion,
Common to all
With the proof
Of God's existence
Resting on faith.
I am inclined to
See goodness in all
With the proof
Of humanity's worth
Resting in faith.
I am inclined to
A desire for peace
For all things created
With the proof
Of hope as a choice
Resting with faith.
I am inclined to
Believing in miracles
Relying on grace
With the proof of blessings
Granted through faith.

November 21, 2002

The Living Will

Sometimes,
I used to wish
That I would die soon,
So that I could be a
Little-Kid-Angel in Heaven.
I wanted to be a Child-Angel
So Jamie, and Katie and Stevie
Would know me
And play with me,
And we could be together
And the same for Forever.
Sometimes,
I also think about
Dying while I am little
Because it's so hard to be
A good person here on earth.
I am afraid that the longer
I am alive, the more I might
Get in trouble, and then I might
Have to sit in Think-Time before
God will let me
Come into Heaven.
But Mommy said that
Even though we make mistakes,
God loves us very much,

And if we are really sorry,
He forgives us and welcomes us
Into His wonderful
Heaven-Home.
We only have to sit in the
Before-Heaven Think-Time if
We are not ready to meet God.
We are the ones who choose
Think-Time, not God.
Mommy also said that
Heaven is so wonderful,
That we can be any age we want.
So even if I don't die until I am
Thirteen or fifty-seven or
One hundred and one years old,
I can still be five years old
In Heaven
If that's what I want to be.
Heaven is anything good
We want it to be.
When I die,
I want to be a
Little-Kid-Angel in Heaven,
But now I know that I don't
Have to die when
I am still a little kid.

March 12, 1996

141

Steps to Heaven

Sometimes,
When I am being very well-behaved,
And people tell me I am doing a good job,
I stop and back up a little bit and think.
When I back up a little bit
It's because I am afraid.
I am afraid that going forward
Will make me actually go back—
Back to Heaven, where I came from.
I want to be good.
I want to know that I'm going forward.
But I don't want to think that I'm going
Too much forward into Heaven too soon.
When I get scared of dying, or of hurting,
I am not as well-behaved, and
I don't do such a good job anymore.
And sometimes, I am even a little nasty.
That makes me sad and confused though.
Even though I am not getting closer to Heaven
When I am nasty and not good,
I am not getting better in living.
I want to go to Heaven, and I want to live.
So I try to behave just enough that
I have to live longer before I can go to Heaven.
But I also try to behave well enough that
If I do die when I am a little kid,
I can still go to Heaven and be with God.

June 22, 1997

142

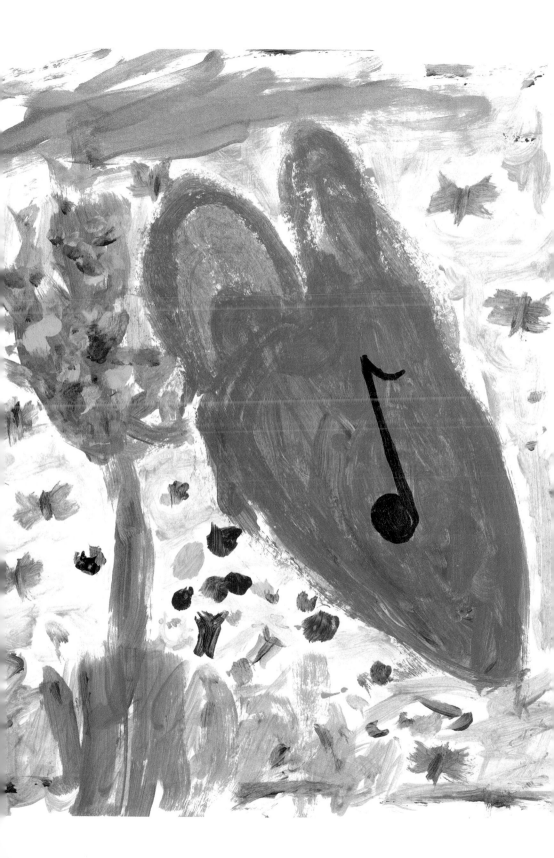

The Dust of God

A long time ago,
I was a leaf on a tree . . .
I was hanging on my tree and
It was during spring
So it rained a lot,
And that was good because I was thirsty.
Then it turned into summer
And it was so hot,
But I felt good when I saw
The beautiful flowers down below.
Then fall came.
I was green, but then I turned red
And fell down to the ground.
When winter came it was cold,
And I began to disappear and turn
Back into the dust that I was made from.
Then spring came again . . .
I was not a tree anymore,
But buried into the ground.
But, I was still a part of
The flowers and of the trees and of
All the life around the world . . .
Because I was the dust that God made,
And that is the dust that God used
To make the whole world, and the animals,
And the plants, and the people.
I am the dust, and
I am the life, and
I am so happy . . .
Hanging on my tree,
Floating to the ground, and
Being the dust of God in the earth.

June 22, 1995

144

Satan's Rocks
Versus God's Shields

Dear God,
Please protect us from
The rocks-of-Satan,
Which are mean words
And evil powers and
Attacks and threats
By people on people.
When Satan's big rock is thrown,
It shatters
Into thousands of tiny pieces.
Each piece has
Pain and anger and hurt,
And when someone
Gets hit with a piece,
They pick it off and
Throw it at someone else . . .
And that is how fights,
And wars, get started.
Dear God,
Help us to see this
Truth in all the badness,
So we do not use
The rocks-of-Satan by just
Throwing them at other
People in anger and hurt.
Thank You for
The Shields-of-Love
That You have given to protect us,
Like courage and respect and
Like wisdom and loyalty.

Dear God,
Thank You for every
Kind person in the world,
Who helps protect the children
Who need it, like me.
Thank You especially
For sharing Your Words,
And for creating the gift of Heaven,
Or else we'd all just lay in the
Ground when we don't need to.
Dear God,
Please help angry people
Understand the true meanings
Of courage and respect and
Of wisdom and loyalty,
And most of all . . . love.
Then they will not think
That power and mean-ness are the
Strongest forces of the universe,
And maybe,
They will stop sending along
All those rocks-of-Satan.
Dear God,
Thank You for all the gifts and
Thank You for all the
Good people You gave us.
Let us use these gifts wisely,
And become even better people,
So that more and more of us
Understand and use
The Shields-of-Love
To defeat the rocks-of-Satan.
Amen.

May 4, 1997

145

Sacred Heartsongs

Bible Lesson for Life

When in anger,
Take not the frustration
Out on God,
Nor on other people.
Do not joke about God
Or God's name disrespectfully,
Nor about other people
Or their names.
That is not the way
God wants us to act
Toward each other.
No matter what
Our faith may be,
We should always remember
To be prayerful and respectful
Of our Creator, and
Of all that has been created.
If we can find peace
In our hearts,
Even in the midst of angry times,
We will be "in the image of God"
As was intended in the beginning.
And that is a valuable lesson
From the heart of the Bible.

April 16, 2000

Rainbow Brothers

When I got picked up
After school one day,
I saw a rainbow.
It went from
Heaven-in-the-sky,
Down to
Heaven-in-the-earth.
When I was a baby,
I saw a rainbow
At my Older-House.
Jamie was on the deck
With me, but
He could not see it
Because his eyes did not work.
He could not smile and clap
With me for the
Beautiful rainbow
Because his body didn't work.
Now, Jamie is in Heaven.
Now, Jamie is with the rainbow.
Now, he doesn't just see the rainbow,
Jamie is with the rainbow.
He can smile and clap
Just like me,
And he can flap his Angel-wings,
And I can flap my real-live-boy arms.
See?
We did the same thing . . .
We are brothers!

March 30, 1994

Psalm for Martin

Have you been
To the mountaintop
And seen the
Goodness of the Lord?

Have you climbed
To the mountaintop
And seen the
Goodness of the Lord?
With His Left hand,
He shall assist you there;
With His Right hand,
He shall greet you.

Have you been
To the mountaintop
And seen the
Goodness of the Lord?

Do not fear the Mountain,
For it is Holy;
The journey is that
Of your life.
When you arrive at the peak,
Look around you,
And see the beauty and
The wonder of God's Creation.

Have you been
To the mountaintop
And seen the
Goodness of the Lord?

Our God will
Always be with us;
Let us rejoice and be glad.
When we are
At the mountaintop,
We can be closer to Him,
And truly see
The work of His hands.

Have you been
To the mountaintop
And seen the
Goodness of the Lord?

Although the journey up the
Mountain may seem difficult,
At the top we will
Hear Our Heartsongs.
Each Heartsong will
Reward and soothe us;
They shall put us in
Harmony with God.

Have you been
To the mountaintop
And seen the
Goodness of the Lord?

September 7, 2001

147

Sacred Heartsongs

The Snow Prayer

Snow . . .
It falls so calmly, yet steadily.
The sound of snow
Is a heavenly silence.
The nature lies still
As it is blessed by the peace . . .
Snow descends to all.
The true gift of snow
Is the love it puts into our spirits.
So cold . . .
Yet putting so much
Warmth in our hearts.
The judgmental, chaotic world
And the children of the
Harsh present who truly need
A better tomorrow
Are still . . .
Are calm . . .
They forget their
Struggles and strife
And play in the today of snow.
The children laugh and hold hands.
The children of all ages, and places
Celebrate in friendship, and
Celebrate in difference,
A devotion to peace . . .
For one moment the world is
Blithe, united, and peaceful.
The snow . . .
Can show us many meanings,
And teach us many lessons
If we open out minds,
And look upon the world with
The heaven-eyes
That perceive from our hearts . . .

The snow is amazing
And the world watches it fall . . .
Swiftly,
Silently,
Filled with a sense of awe,
And wonder,
Of such a wonderful, blessed gift.
We notice,
In silence . . .
The stillness of the earth.
All of God's great Creation
Wonders and notices in senses
Which are only felt
When an amazing grace
Descends to us from Heaven.
That amazing grace of snow
Gives us hope and joy . . .
No matter who,
Or what,
Or where,
Or how,
Or even why
We are . . .
Lions and lambs,
Rivals and friends,
Are still . . .
Are noticing . . .
Are joyous . . .
Are peaceful . . .
In the graceful,
Falling,
Silent,
Amazing,
And ever-giving snow.

December 24, 2002

148

Window into Heaven

Once, when I was a little-bitty baby,
I went into Heaven.
Really I did.
I went through the window
That goes into the Heaven-in-the-sky,
And I was really in Heaven.
I saw my sister, Katie, and my brother, Stevie,
But I didn't see my brother, Jamie, in Heaven.
I didn't know how to talk yet,
But I said hello to Katie and Stevie
And we were very happy to be together again.
But then,
I had to come back through the window
And leave Heaven.
And then,
I was a little-bitty baby Mattie again.
I miss Katie and Stevie.
I didn't used to miss Jamie, because he used to be
Here with me, and not in Heaven.
But now,
I miss Jamie, too.
I don't want to die like my brother, Jamie,
Or like Katie and Stevie.
But I want to go back to Heaven again.
And now,
I know how to talk because I am a big boy.
I want to be with God, and with Katie and Stevie.
And I want to be with Jamie.
I don't want to die, yet,
But I want to go through the window
Into the Heaven-in-the-sky
To be happy with them again.

February 1, 1994

149

Sacred Heartsongs

Planning for the Future

Heaven is a wonderful place.
When a good-hearted person dies,
His or her spirit rises into Heaven.
And, Heaven is a forever place
That transcends our mortal
Sense of time and space.
There can be many different
Views on what Heaven is like,
Because Heaven is whatever
Makes each person
Eternally and fully happy.
To go to Heaven,
A person must be
Pure in heart, and truly sorry
For any sins committed.
If a person is not clean in heart
When he or she dies,
That person might have
To think and better prepare
For the eternal wonders of Heaven.
So, we should live each moment
Of life in a state of readiness,
And peaceful grace.

April 3, 2000

The Carpenter and the Angel

I've been told
Their names are John and Kathy.
I've been told
Their roles are to help the campers.
I've been told
Their hopes are to make a difference.
I know what
I've been told
But all the same,
I know what I believe . . .
That these two are really
The Carpenter and the Angel.

June 19, 2002

150

The Last Night

Last night, I had a dream.
A spectacular dream.
An enchanting dream.
A vision of a dream to be true.
Last night, I had a dream
In which a lovely angel,
Gentle and light,
Came with the dawning sky,
Dancing, hovering, guarding,
Above the cabins of camp.
And from each cabin
Rose a namesake bird . . .
A robin from Robin,
A wren from Wren,
A lark from Lark,
A namesake bird tor
Each of the dozen cabins.
And they danced and played
With the hovering guardian
Angel of loveliness.
There was music, though
A melody too perfect
In a dream to recall.

It was a celebration
Of life.
Of being.
Of friends
Helping friends.
And then,
I awoke from this
Spectacular, enchanting
Vision of a dream,
Giving praise.
Giving praise for
Being here in body
As well as in spirit.
Giving praise for
Another year
Of summer camp.
Giving praise for
The reverent reality
Of angels
In dreams and
In wakes and
In front of you
In life,
When you have
The vision to look.

June 22, 2002

Sacred Heartsongs

The Church Ride

Sometimes,
I think that there should be a very special
Carnival ride, that is all about church.
All of the people will go inside
The church and sit in the pews.
We will hear a voice on the loudspeaker
That will say, "Buckle your seat belts."
After everyone buckles up,
We will hear a loud boom-click,
And the doors will be shut tight,
And lock us in from the outside.
And then the voice will say,
"Your journey is about to begin."
And the church will rise up
And spin and zoom and whirl all around . . .
And everyone will not know for sure
Whether they are excited, or scared.
And suddenly,
We will see light all around,
And Angels singing "Alleluia!"
And we will feel so happy and good,
And there will be nothing that we want.
The voice on the loudspeaker will say,
"This is Heaven, folks. Heaven is a wonderful place!"
And the people on the ride will sing
"Alleluia" with the Angels,
And with the each-other people on the ride,
And with the people in Heaven
Who we used to know when they were alive.

152

But then,
The church will start to spin and zoom and whirl
All around again, and it will get so windy and dark . . .
And windy and dark, and the
Light of the Angels will disappear.
And we will look out and see all of the devils,
And we will be sad and afraid.
The devils will be laughing like the Angels,
But it will be mean and nasty laughing without any "Alleluias."
And we will all scream out, "Help us! Help us!
How do we get back to life? Help us!"
And the voice on the loudspeaker will say,
"Follow the good. Follow the good people,
And follow the good light,
And follow the good laughing sounds.
Do not follow the bad, even if you hear laughing.
It is not happy laughing.
It is your choice, but to get back to life,
Follow the good, people, follow the good!"
And the Church Ride will begin
To go back down to Earth . . .
And it will land safely where it began.
The seat belts will unbuckle,
The doors will unlock,
And the voice on the loudspeaker will say,
"Welcome back. I hope you have enjoyed your journey.
Do not forget this ride, ever.
Good bye, and have a good life."
And we will each leave the Church Ride,
And go through the doors, to make our choice.

June 4, 1995

153

Angel Words (II)

Last night,
I felt my Guardian Angel.
And my Angel said
Into my heart,
"Glory to God in the highest,
And on Earth,
Peace to all children.
And peace to all countries,
And states,
And colors of skin."
That's what my Angel said.
And then Katie and Stevie and Jamie
And all of the Angels
And Kings in Heaven,
Like Jesus and Martin Luther,
Smiled at my Angel,
And let a star shine down
Onto my house, and
Onto my family, and
Onto my self.
And for this,
I thank You, God.
And of this,
Is my prayer tonight.
Amen.

January 15, 1995

Tao de Heartsongs

When one person
Is thoughtful to another,
The thoughtfulness
Gets carried on and on.
It is like a great river of kindness,
Once blocked by rocks,
That is suddenly opened
By a single person's
Kind thought or act . . .

Excerpt from "Flowing Thoughtfulness"
by Mattie J.T. Stepanek, in *Loving Through Heartsongs*
(Hyperion/VSP, 2003)

PREVIOUS PAGE: Mattie in his "peace" outfit for a school performance, spring 1999

TOP: Mattie enjoying the autumn colors, fall 1999

BOTTOM LEFT: Mattie offering flowers and a prayer, spring 1998

BOTTOM RIGHT: Mattie just after earning his Black Belt, summer 1998

In my seventy-one years as an entertainer, I've been blessed to know many great people—from physicians, to scientists, to performers, to world leaders—who had tremendous passion about what they did. When it comes to brilliance and accomplishment and creativity, I thought I'd pretty much seen it all. Then sometime last year I was given a book called Heartsongs by a young person named Mattie Stepanek.

At first I was curious about Mattie's poetry because I knew he was affected by one of the diseases we at the Muscular Dystrophy Association are dedicated to defeating. When I began to read Mattie's words, I was stunned. They stirred feelings inside of me that I hadn't known existed. I found myself wondering, "Is this real? Can it be that a child of this age knows so much about love and life and spirituality?" Mattie's words had such magnificent depth and sensitivity that I felt they could only have come from a mind like that of Carl Sandburg or even Elie Wiesel. But then I read on and said to myself, "There has never been a mind quite like Mattie's." The real joy was when I read some of the book with my ten-year-old daughter, Danielle. Mattie's poems are not just meant to be read, but to be shared.

I am so proud to have Mattie working alongside me as MDA National Goodwill Ambassador. He's such an illuminating force—I thank God every day for the passion he brings to this urgent mission, which is fully equal to the intensity he brings to his brilliant poetry. And that is saying a lot.[1] . . .

What Mattie means to me is he is the elixir for all of the poisons out there. When you have the naysayers, when you have the people that break your heart because they come and they send you an e-mail [saying] how much money do you get from the telethon? And they break your heart with this kind of stupidity, then I've got Mattie, who looks at me as he did, when we were with the firefighters in Vegas. I gave him a hug when I had to leave, and he held me and didn't let the hug be quick. And when I did pull away he said, "That was the greatest hug I've ever had in my whole life."[2] . . .

Mattie was something special, something very special. His example made people want to reach for the best within themselves. It was easy to forget how sick he was because his megawatt personality just made you want to smile.[3]

—Jerry Lewis

(National Chairperson, Muscular Dystrophy Associaton)

From excerpts by Jerry Lewis
1. Foreword to *Celebrate Through Heartsongs* by Mattie J.T. Stepanek (Hyperion/VSP, 2002).
2. MDA Labor Day Telethon 2002.
3. *Larry King Live*, September 2004.

157

When Mattie was four years old, he began taking "Hapkido," a martial art that encourages self-discipline, respect for others and the world, and self-defense rather than attack for personal safety. As he learned balance, motor coordination, and Korean phrases, he also practiced patience, meditation, humility, and other strengths of character. Mattie took pride in every color belt and in every trophy he earned on the journey toward his First Degree Black Belt. But what mattered most to Mattie during his years of training, and during his opportunities for teaching Hapkido to newer students, was the very first lesson he was ever given by his Grandmaster: "Why do we study Hapkido? To become a better person."

Mattie witnessed a world scattered with sadness, anger, fear, need, desire, and other inevitable conditions of the human body, mind, and spirit. Yet, he believed that people, and life, were inherently good and worthy. He held the conviction that peace—for one's self and for one's world—is possible if we each live as the best person we can be, and if we recognize and embrace opportunities to help every other person also live fully. The beautiful gift of humanity is realized when each individual strives to make a gentle, positive, and recurring difference for others.

In this chapter, Tao de Heartsongs, the reader finds poetry that explores "the way of" Mattie's thinking, believing, and living. We appreciate a child who celebrated the gift of "being alive" and who lived with a purpose, and for a purpose. Whether the topic is giggling, grieving, or growing older, or playing, praying, or peacemaking, these poems portray the art of treasuring both the ordinary and the extraordinary blessings of daily life.

Hearing Is Believing

Not everyone realizes this, but
Everyone makes poetry.
Even if people don't sit down
And write or say out the poems,
We all have poetry in our hearts.
We each have a song inside our heart
That can make peace in the world,
If we first make peace inside ourselves.
Hearing and understanding about
The importance of our Heartsongs Is easy.
The hard part is believing in Heartsongs,
Especially if you are a grown-up
Who hasn't listened to one for a long time.
That's okay, though, because anyone who
Really, really wants to understand about
Heartsongs can just ask a friend,
Or a child, to share their poetry with them
And once you've heard a Heartsong again,
You will remember, and believe again,
And begin to make your own poetry for life.

June 20, 1997

Passages

When I was a little-bitty baby,
Before I turned two-and-then-three,
I had a trach.
I could only say "Aaaaa"
With my mouth,
But I could say lots of words
With my hands.
I wore diapers,
And drank from a bottle.
I slept in a crib
With my Mr. Bunny and Binky.
Now I am a big boy,
Because I am three-and-a-half.
I don't have a trach anymore,
But I still have my heart monitor,
And my red light machines.
I can say lots and lots of
Words with my mouth,
But I still remember my
Sign Language, too.
I wear big boy underpants,
And I drink from a cup and a straw.
I sleep in my big boy Jamie-bed,
And I don't suck on my Binky . . .
But I still hug Mr. Bunny,
And need to be held and rocked.

October 1, 1993

About Birthstones

Everybody is born in a month.
And every month has a birthstone.
Some are sparkling gems,
All white or golden or silvery.
Mommy and I were born
In the month of rubies—
Pinkish red, wonderful and alive,
Like a sunset over the water.
My brothers were born
In the months of sky colors—
Bright and dark purple and blue,
Twinkling the happiness of cherubs.
My sister was born
In the month of gentle blue—
Shining, glimmering calm,
Tenderly like Heaven on earth.
All of the birthstones are beautiful,
Because all people are born beautiful.
But sometimes,
A person does not live beautiful inside.
And then, the gift of a birthstone
Turns into a plain and ugly rock,
Or a petrified fossil of something.
It's sad, but I know someone
Who is so angry that his birthstone
Is just a shriveled-up hickory nut.

October 10, 1997

Tao de Heartsongs

On Growing Up (Part II)

In Peter Pan stories,
The Lost Boys and Peter
Live in Neverland,
So that they don't
Ever have to grow up.
Sometimes,
That sounds nice and fun.
I like being a little kid, and
Playing and learning
And all that type of stuff.
But I still want to grow up.
I thought I might like to
Go to Neverland, to visit.
But I would never stay there.
I want to have birthdays.
I want to grow older.
I want to get married.
I want to go to work.
I want to be a peacemaker.

To do all those things means
I can't go to Neverland
Because I *need* to grow up.
And you know what?
I can still have all the fun
Of being a kid
When I grow up,
Because I will have children
And be a daddy.
That means I
Can play with them,
And read to them,
And learn with them,
And run with them,
And take them places,
And give them my old toys,
And teach them peace,
And have all kinds of fun.
You don't have to stay
Little to have fun.
All you have to do is play
And be happy about things!

January 16, 1996

Tao de Heartsongs

On Growing Up (Part IV)

After all the poems of growing up,
This is a new lesson of growing up.
Now this lesson is important like the others,
But it's not just "growing" up
That is important.
It's also learning to work hard and
Get jobs so that we can have money.
Because if we didn't have money,
We couldn't get food, and
Then we would starve, and die.
But we are lucky that we get jobs
And get money for the jobs
So we can have good food, and live,
Instead of having sad death, and dying.
It may sound easy, but it's not.
It's hard, because some countries
Don't have jobs, and they
Don't have food, and they
Do have wars,
And the people die.
So *this* is the lesson about growing up—
Learn to work to earn money for food,
But it's even more important to
Learn to work together, so we can live.
If we work with each other,
There will be no war.
So whenever there's work to do,
Make sure that you do it together,
So there will be no wars,
And there will be more jobs,
And there will be more food,
And people will live without dying!

August 23, 1996

162

The Usefulness of Regression

Maybe today
I will turn back
Into a little-bitty baby.
I will crawl around
And say, "Goo-goo" and
"Gah-gah" and "gootchie goo."
My mommy will have to
Carry me around and
Feed me with a bottle and spoon.
And that means my mommy
Will have to learn to
Stand up and walk again.
I will help her.
Then she can run
And she can play with me
Just like we used to when
I was a little baby.
And no big kids will
Laugh at me or hit me or
Kick me or push me.
And if they call me "Baby"
It will be okay
Because I really will be a baby,
Not a little big boy
Who falls down so much
And who can't do all those
Things that the big boys do.
I will just crawl
Into my mommy's lap
And say "Goo-goo."
It's amazing what a
Little baby talk can do.

October 12, 1994

About Feelings

Some things hurt my feelings,
Like when other people tease me.
I have been teased by kids
About my oxygen, and
About not being able to keep up.
I have even been teased by kids
For not teasing other kids,
And for setting a moral example.
I have been teased by someone
For not keeping scary secrets,
And for being afraid
Of threatening things.
I have even been teased
By someone who knew better
About having a disability.
When things hurt my feelings,
Usually I try to talk
To the person who has hurt me.
Sometimes, I have to talk
To a person I trust instead.
It is important for people
To be honest
When expressing themselves.
But, it is also important to be
Always thoughtful and considerate
In expressing feelings to others,
So that more feelings are not hurt.

March 14, 2000

About Basic Information

When I meet new people,
There are all kinds of different
Things I can tell them about.
I can tell them that
Being smart isn't just knowing
ABCs and numbers.
It's also paying attention and
Listening and knowing
How to combine
Your body power and
Your mind power.
I can tell them about
Something new,
Like my oxygen tank.
I have kind of a
Breathing problem,
And the oxygen keeps
My muscles strong.
Sometimes the tank goes "Ooooooo-h"
When it is full, and it doesn't
Go like that when it's not full.
And I can tell them about
Being alive and dead.
I can say about
Katie and Stevie
Who were born and died
Before Jamie and me,
And we never
Even knew them.

And then Jamie died,
But I didn't,
Even though we had
The same machines
To help us breathe and
The same doctor.
I can say about how sad it is
To miss someone,
And how it's hard to
Understand all about it,
And how sometimes
It even makes you feel
Angry or silly or confused
Or anything,
Or even nothing at all.
But if you tell about it,
Or write about it,
It helps you
Feel better about it
Until it hurts again.
Yes, those are
Some of the different things
I can tell new people
When I meet them.
I will tell them about wisdom,
I will tell them about oxygen, and
I will tell them about
How brothers and sisters die.

December 12, 1995

Sincere Prayers

Dear God,
Thank You for taking such good care
Of my brother, Jamie.
And if I cry sometimes, God,
Because I miss my brother so much,
Remember that that's okay.
Whining is not good, but
It's alright to cry.
And God,
You can cry, too,
And that's okay.
Crying gets the mad
And the sad out of you.
So thank You, God,
For my tears to help feel me better.
Oh, and God? . . .
If you see a monster in my room,
Well, if you'd please get it out,
I'll thank You for that, too.
And all this I pray
Through Jamie my Jamie
And God our Creator
For Mattie this little boy.
Amen.

August 22, 1994

Preschool Medicine

I get to go to Hapkido practice
And learn to get all different color belts.
But Mommy can't take Hapkido
Because her muscles don't work well.
So, when I grow up,
I will be a doctor,
And I will fix my mommy's muscles.
I will probably have to give her
Shots and needles.
They will really hurt a lot,
But only for a minute.
I won't give them because I am angry,
Or because she did something wrong.
I will give them because they have
Special medicine
That will make her all better.
I will hold her hand
To help her be brave,
And Katie, Stevie, and Jamie will
Put their Angel-hands on her shoulder
To help her also.
We will all be so proud of our mommy.
And then,
The Angels will put
A star on the crown in her heart,
And Mattie and Mommy
Can run and play together again,
Just like when Mattie was a little baby.

January 14, 1995

165

Tao de Heartsongs

"Yes, God"

It's very important
To eat nutritious food.
It helps you
To grow stronger and
To live longer.
Junk food tastes good,
But it's not nutritious
And it doesn't help you
Meditate better,
So you should only
Eat a little bit of
The junk food for fun.
I want to live a very,
Very, very long time.
So I eat lots of
Vegetables and fruits and
Only a little junk food,
Unless it's nutritious
Junk food that has
Vegetables in it like
Popcorn or potato chips.
But I know that one day,
God will call to me,
And ask me to join Him
In the Forever
And Wonderful Heaven.

And when He calls me,
Even if I am young or old,
I will say to Him,
"Yes, God.
I will come to You."
And then I will rise
Just like Jesus did,
And like the prophets did,
And like Jamie did,
And like Katie and Stevie did,
And like Martin Luther King did,
And like all the
Other good people did.
And then,
I will never be hurt or sick
Or slow or teased or sad again.
I won't even have
This body anymore,
Because my
Muscles-and-bones will
Be all dead and buried,
And my spirit will be so happy.

May 9, 1995

It's a Bumpy Ride Through Life

A bump means trouble, and
A bump means a problem, and
A bump means we're
Traveling through life.
On a smooth road,
Our troubles are over
For a while, and we can
Live quietly, gently, peacefully.
But life is 50/50, when it's good.
There are rough times
When we must hold on tight
Or we'll fall out,
Or we'll hurt ourselves,
Or we'll get taken away,
Or we'll die.
During the bumpy times,
I hold on by praying, and
By listening to my Heartsongs.
When the road is smooth,
And I can sit back and relax,
And enjoy my life and play,
I enjoy my life by praying, and
By sharing my Heartsongs.
It's a bumpy ride through life—
Through rough times and
Through smooth times.
And even though the ride is bumpy
And it may get sad and hard,
There are lessons—
The bumpy ride teaches us
Something, somehow,
If we travel it with our Heartsongs.

November 19, 1998

About Procreation

Life is a great gift
Given to us by God.
With that gift,
We are given the ability
To continue giving life
To future generations
Through procreation.
Without this special ability,
People could not multiply,
And human life would end.
And then,
God would be lonely again,
As it was before
The creation of humans.
Even though it is good to give life,
We shouldn't ever toy
With life in a bad way.
We should never threaten a life.
Nor should we ever use the gift
Of procreation inappropriately.
The more we bring beautiful
Lives into this world,
The more we bring opportunities
For friendship into the world.
Some day, I hope to be
A part of that opportunity,
Through God's gift of life.

May 7, 2000

The Gifts of a Mother

Beginning with the time
Her baby is born,
A mother cares
For her offspring
With all of her heart,
And commences the journey
Of giving so many gifts.
During birth,
A mother gives
Life to her baby,
Even while aware of
The waiting challenges,
Through the gift
Of eternal love.
During infancy,
A mother feeds,
Loves, and protects,
Yet at the same time, introduces
Her growing child to the world
Through the gift
Of encouraged curiosity.
During childhood,
A mother teaches
Many wise lessons,
And how to live a good life,
Through the gift
Of inspired learning.
During adolescence,
A mother advocates
Safety and ongoing honesty,
And how to study
Hard for the future,

Through the gift
Of mutual respect.
During adulthood,
A mother supports
Independence,
And gracefully allows
Her child to move on,
Through the gift
Of enduring confidence.
All of these gifts that
A mother gives to her child
Through life
Create the future as it might be,
Filled with
Peaceful and confident
Endurance,
Healthy and respectful
Honesty,
Happy and inspiring
Growth,
Hopeful and encouraged
Curiosity,
And most of all . . .
An eternal love
For life and future.

May 18, 2000

168

Feelings on Friendship

Whether a person
Has one friend
Or more than
One hundred friends
Does not matter.
What does matter
Is that each person
Experiences the
Pleasure and
Bonding of friendship.
Friends keep
Each other company.
They play with each other.
They help each other.
They support each other
During difficult times.
A friend is someone
To share with,
And friends are people
Who care for each other.
And while people can have
Many, many
Friends through life,
It is wonderful to have
A few best friends,
Who are very close in spirit.

When with a friend,
People must remember
The priceless
Value of the bond.
Friends should never
Be mean or thoughtless,
Or let anger
Break up a friendship.
Friendships
Are more important than
Winning a disagreement.
If people remember to
"Do unto others as they want
Others to do unto them,"
And not just return what's
Been hurtfully
Done unto them,
Friendships will grow
Gently and smoothly,
And people will feel
A peace in their spirits.
And the more
Friendship and peace
Flows through the world,
The more we create
A better future for life.

June 1, 2000

The MDA Research Minute

The MDA Research Minute . . .
Our bulldozer, our torch.
Our fight, our hope.
Our victory, our celebration.

The MDA Research Minute . . .
Challenges that seem
Unconquerable,
Obstacles that seem
Insurmountable,
Are plowed down,
Rolled over,
Paving a smoother road
For the journey.

The MDA Research Minute . . .
A flicker of insight
Burning bright with desire,
And desperation,
Dances us into the future,
Transforming the passive
Wish for cures
Into active
Hope for understanding
That will rid us of
The last ashes of
Neuromuscular disease.

Just think on the reality of
The MDA Research Minute . . .

The minute it takes
To read these lines
Costs a fortune in the labs
Dedicated
To reading between the lines
Of medical mysteries.
It is the human touch
That lights our path,
Fueling the
Energy and momentum.
The greater the touch,
The brighter the torch,
The brighter the torch,
The stronger the energy.

The MDA Research Minute . . .
Just think on the reality.
Just think, and be . . .
Be a part of the
MDA Research Minute.
Be a part of the bulldozer.
Be a part of the torch.
Be a part of the energy . . .
And be a hero for our reality.

February 15, 2003

170

Mourning Thoughts

Hi Jamie!
It's me, Mattie.
I am going to school now.
I used to
Give you a toy before school,
But, now you're in Heaven,
And I can't.
Remember when
We came to visit you at the
Cemetery-part-of-Heaven?
I do, too.
I miss you, Jamie . . .
I can't see you,
Or hear you,
Or touch you anymore.
But I can talk to you,
And pray to you,
And think of you.
I remember you.
And I drew my Jamie
A rainbow yesterday, too.
Now, you are smiling
In Heaven, Jamie.
See? . . .
Just like before you died . . .
I made you smile
Before I went to school.
I love you, Jamie.
I love you very much,
And Forever,
Just like Heaven-Forever.
I'm glad you are
Happy in Heaven . . .
And now,
Heaven is happy, too.

September 16, 1993

Sometimes . . .

Sometimes
We eat ice cream . . .
And sometimes
We don't eat ice cream.
Sometimes
We do puzzles . . .
And sometimes
We don't do puzzles.
Sometimes
We play upside-down . . .
And sometimes
We don't play upside-down.
Sometimes
We take a bath . . .
And sometimes
We don't take a bath.
Sometimes
We share nicely . . .
And sometimes
We don't share nicely.
Sometimes
We do good listening . . .
And sometimes
We don't do good listening.
Sometimes
We feel sad and angry . . .
And sometimes
We don't feel sad and angry.
Sometimes
We miss Jamie . . .
And sometimes
We don't miss Jamie.

September 17, 1993

Tao de Heartsongs

Innocent Thoughts, Innocent Hopes

Do you know
What is one of the saddest things
Someone can say to someone else?
"You will never see
The light of another day!"
That's what Scar says in *The Lion King*.
That meant that he wanted The Mouse to die.
If you're a good listener, and
If you have God in your heart
While you're alive,
You go to Heaven when you die,
And that is wonderful.
But you're not supposed to die
Just because someone else is mean,
Or because someone else
Wants you to die.
You're only supposed to die
When the muscles-and-bones
That God gave you
Really don't work anymore,
Even though you loved them
And took good care of them
Because they were a gift from God.
So, isn't that sad about what Scar said?
Isn't it so sad that someone
Would want someone else to die?
Isn't it so sad that lots of
Little children and other people
Get killed when people
Shoot them or hurt them?
Isn't it so sad that Hitler
Killed all those people
Because they prayed to God
With different words and

172

In a different church?
Isn't it so sad that
Martin Luther King got killed
Because someone didn't like
The color skin God gave him?
Isn't it so sad that Jesus got killed
Because He tried to teach us
About God and about how
To be good listeners?
I know Easter is fun to celebrate
Because now we have Heaven,
But I still think that it's all
A little bit sad that some people
Cut down a dogwood tree
And nailed such a good person to it.
I think Jesus maybe wanted to
Stay here with his friends longer.
I want to see
The light of another day.
And so do lots and lots
Of other children and people.
The little Mouse got away from Scar,
And that is very good.
But how can we get people to
Stop being so nasty to each other?
Maybe everyone needs to learn to meditate,
And combine their mind and body and spirit.
Then, maybe
People would start to think
About what they say and what they do.
And then, maybe nobody else would get killed.
They would only die when their bodies don't work
And it's time for their spirits to go to Heaven,
Just like God wants it to be.

April 21, 1995

173

Literal Follower

Jesus said that whoever is
First on earth will be
Last in Heaven,
And whoever is
Last on earth will be
First in Heaven.
I used to try to
Always be first in line
Because I like being leader.
I would race to the front,
And sometimes,
I even pushed to the front.
From now on,
I will race to the back,
And I guess if I have to,
I will push to the back,
Because I'd rather be
First in Heaven for my Forever,
And last on earth for my now.

March 5, 1996

Important Things (II)

Life is very busy.
Every day, we are
Teaching,
Learning,
Working,
Cleaning,
Eating,
Sleeping,
Giving,
Taking,
Wondering,
Trying,
Being, and
Doing so many
Different things.
But, we should
Always remember
To take time for
The most important
Things in life . . .
Playing and Praying.

April 30, 2000

174

Opportunity Knocking

I open the door
To each new day.
I welcome the dawn and
I swing open wide
The entry portal
To each next moment in life.
Some days thrust tsunamis
With storms and squalls.
Some days shower sunshine
With laughter and love.
Some days illustrate
The circle of life,
Highlighting the grass which
Is always greener
On the other side of the hills
Where blossoms grow and
The land prospers
Fruitfully and the
Dreams always come true,
Or perhaps,

They don't really
Stand a chance.
As birds announce life
Through sweet or sad songs
Of that part of the circle
Which cannot be seen
From this side,
I walk with content
In the green of my youth,
Though shaded with challenges,
Each darkened or lightened by
My choices in vision and views.
But I know that if only
I open my eyes and
I open my mind and
I open my life,
I open the door
To each new day.

April 7, 2002

175

If My Arms Were as Long as a Rainbow

If my arms were as long as a rainbow,
I would be able to reach all around the whole house,
And maybe even up through the rooftop.
If my arms were as long as a rainbow,
I would be able to reach around the whole neighborhood,
And deep into the woods.
If my arms were as long as a big rainbow,
I would be able to reach up the trees and down again,
And all the way to the sun and the moon and the stars
That shine so brightly onto our Earth.
And if my arms were as long as the biggest rainbow ever . . .
I would be able to reach all around the whole world!
If I could reach around the whole world,
And around the sun and the moon and the stars,
And around the neighborhood and the house,
I would lift them all up and together into Heaven,
So that all the people of earth and of Heaven
Could hug and kiss each other.
But, my arms aren't really that long,
So the only way I can hug and kiss the whole world
Is by closing my eyes,
And reaching out with my mind,
And believing in my Heartsongs,
And sharing them with everyone and everything.
So in the end,
We know that our arms and our minds and our hearts
Are all as big as we believe them to be,
Which might just be as long as a rainbow.

October 16, 1996

Recipe for Peace

Peace is possible.
Make peace an attitude.
Want it.
Make peace a habit.
Live it.
Make peace a reality.
Share it.
Peace is possible.
Make peace matter.
Our matter.
Make peace a priority.
Our priority.
Make peace a choice.
Our choice.
Peace is possible.

We must
Think gently,
Speak gently,
Live gently.
Peace is possible.
Be happy with who you are.
Be happy with who others are.
Be happy that we Are.
Peace is possible.
Role model acceptance.
Love others.
Role model forgiveness.
Encourage others.
Role model tolerance.
Treasure others.
Peace is possible.
Peace is possible.
Peace is possible.

May 12, 2002

177

On Meditation

To meditate . . .
To really, really meditate,
You must believe from your heart.
You must be in your heart.
When you meditate,
You must try not to lose it.
You do this by not thinking about it,
Only you think hard
From inside your mind and heart.
You must believe
You can stay in the meditation,
And hold on and don't let go, but
Without staying or holding on or letting go at all.
You must feel and
Believe in your own meditation,
Tighter and tighter and tighter . . .
Think about the past,
Think about the present,
Think about the future,
And be, right now, with all of them,
And also, with none of them at all.
Think about when you were younger.
Think about where you were older.
Think about anything, but
Believe in it as you think,
And don't touch it,
But don't let it go.
Meditation helps you rest,
But also think when you rest
So that you get energy to be stronger.
Like when you think about the wind
And the song that the wind sings to you.
The leaves whoosh
And sing with the branches,

Tao de Heartsongs

And the branches of trees
Then sing with the rain.
The song of the air,
In the wind or the stillness,
Is like the song of the breathing of people—
Ones who you love
And ones who love you,
One who you loved
And they died but they live—
Think about them,
Think about the wind of life,
And never let go . . .
Think lighter and lighter and lighter . . .
The lighter you get,
The more the meditation stops
And you are out of the meditation,
But still thinking.
You are like a feather,
Floating out of yourself,
And into the wind-song,
The life-song,
The Heartsong.
And then, when you are finished,
You come back down into yourself,
Your mind,
Your heart.
You come back,
And put down your meditation time.
Maybe write about it,
Maybe think about it some more.
But don't lose it from your life.
And then, you can meditate again,
Whenever you want,
And be rested and thoughtful, and stronger.

November 1, 1996

179

Tao de Heartsongs

Three Spirit Wishes

Wish One:
I wish that all the
War would stop.
I made this wish because
I don't want World War III.
It will blow up the earth.
Wish Two:
I wish I could
Go to Heaven.
I made this wish because
I want to see Jamie,
And Katie and Stevie.
Wish Three:
I wish that I will
Become a remembered writer.
I made this wish because
It's one of my greatest dreams.
I want to be a Peacemaker and
An Ambassador of Humanity.
My life would be different
If any of my Three Wishes
Really ever came true,
Especially Wish Two.
It would change my life
By getting my family
Back together with
My mommy and me.
That is why this wish
Is also my greatest prayer.

March 6, 1998

180

The Will of the Spirit

When I got really scared
About the changes in my life,
I wrote out a will.
I willed my collectible cards
And my stuffed animals
To my friends.
I willed my books and my poetry
To my mom.
I willed my trophies
To Grandmaster Lee.
But, I never willed
My Black Belt to anyone.
That is because
My Black Belt is in my heart,
Which is the connection between
The body and mind and the spirit.
And so, Hapkido will always
Be a part of my future,
And I will always
Be loyal to those
Who have inspired that future.
One day, I might live
To be a Grandmaster.
I will spread my energy
And optimism to others,
Just like it has been spread to me.
My sharing will be
My way of thanking everyone
For the lessons,
For the energy,
And for the future.

February 5, 2000

181

About Hope

Hope is a garden
Of seeds sown with tears,
Planted with love
Amidst present fears.

Hope is a rainbow
Of butterfly wings,
Gently it beckons,
Lightly it sings.

Hope is a present
Of future each day,
A voice from our heart
To show us the way.

Hope is not passive,
It's real and alive,
Hope is a strength
To guide choices made wise.

Yes, hope is a garden
Grown from love and from tears,
And hope which is nurtured
Survives throughout years.

May 21, 2003

Final Heartsongs

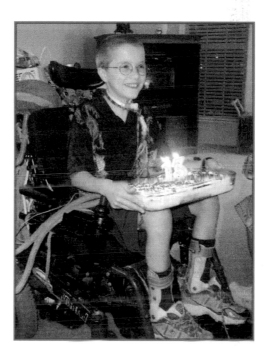

And so for now,
When I swing,
I move back and forth
In the everywhere
And the nowhere
That is the understanding
Of an echo—
The echo of my spirit
That grows from my life,
And that sounds like
A peaceful, but lonely cry,
For the times
When I swing
Before I die.

Excerpt from "Future Echo" by Mattie J.T. Stepanek,
in *Journey Through Heartsongs* (Hyperion/VSP, 2002)

PREVIOUS PAGE: Mattie celebrates his thirteenth birthday, July 2003

TOP LEFT: Mattie with his service dog, Micah, December 2003

TOP RIGHT: Mattie and "Gollum" from *Lord of the Rings*, Christmas 2003

BOTTOM: Mattie at one of his last book signings, December 2003

When I first pitched the profile of a child poet suffering from a rare disease, it was for a series on "great stories of survival" [for ABC's Good Morning America]. The pitch was rejected. Mattie Stepanek was seen as someone who was dying and, therefore, not a survivor. Of course, nothing could be further from the truth. This boy was all about surviving, and not merely outliving. Mattie was coming in to his own just as the country was reeling from the 9/11 attacks. It was a time that the country was lost in an unprecedented level of uncertainty about survival on all levels: as a nation, as a world power, as individuals. And here was this boy on the brink himself, connected to tubes that controlled his fate in a fight against something that anyone who knew anything had said was unwinnable long ago . . . and he was smiling.

His life was about more than a heartbeat, it was about a message of enduring value. This fragile little boy was telling people to be strong, to learn to play after every storm; a boy suffering from an incurable disease who asked others to have hope . . . He was the manifestation of uncommon wisdom coming out of the mouths of babes. He was a survivor; not because of the outcome, but because of the struggle and the optimism and the love he gave to all those around him. And each time he appeared, each time he wrote or spoke to a group, each time he battled back from the brink, he reinforced his message and the understanding that he was a survivor.

But when I first heard of this little man, he and his message were largely unknown. After some prodding my bosses agreed to do a profile on Mattie . . . and once people saw him, heard his poetry and absorbed the simple instructions about life and love . . . he was embraced not only by the show, but by the country . . . for his message, and for his magical survival.

—Chris Cuomo
(Emmy Award-Winning Correspondent,
Primetime Thursday and *Good Morning America*)

Excerpts from Tribute to Mattie by Chris Cuomo during the Third Annual Heartsongs Luncheon to benefit Children's National Medical Center, February 2005, Bethesda, Maryland

Final Heartsongs

Mattie's earliest year of creating poetry was rooted in powerful issues for a young child—balancing the realization and consideration of mortality and spirituality, while discovering and celebrating the gifts of creation that span the two. Mattie's last year of life began with the funeral of a dear friend who died from a neuromuscular disease at the age of fifteen. Not the same neuromuscular disease that shortened Mattie's life and the lives of his three siblings, but the same one that led to the death of her younger sister two years earlier. And so, in his final year of creating poetry, Mattie was still contending with the same intense and prevailing realities—loving people and life, losing siblings and friends, and looking for meaning in the here and now, and in something bigger and better than the here and now.

The selections in this chapter, Final Heartsongs, reveal essential aspects of Mattie's thinking and understanding as he feels the "near distance of Life in his life." While some of these poems impart inevitable images of frustration, desperation, even lonely resignation during his journey, others seek and find consolation, inspiration, even excited anticipation for the wonders of Eternity. In reflecting on these expressions as a portrait through Heartsongs, no reader will be surprised to see the simplicity of a child who witnessed and wrote about cherishing life from ages three to thirteen, nor the profound meditations of a young man who spent his entire "almost fourteen years" giving voice to his view of Life from the edge.

It is never okay when a child dies, even when the child looks death square in the eye and reckons with its reality, its eventuality, and its finality. At some level, we want to know, or to glimpse at the intensity of such insights, at least through the distance of the written word. Yet at the same time, we are not comfortable entering such sadness, such truth. But these poems are not morbid, and the greatest gift in this chapter is that Mattie triumphs.

True, Mattie's mortal life ended, and he was both blessed and burdened with awareness of the approach. But he believed that how we touch the world in each moment truly matters. And, he believed that we have opportunities to create our own epitaph and legacy, the echo and silhouette of our lives, if we choose to live gently, and genuinely, and graciously. Thus, Mattie was able to believe in the message of hope and peace that he offered the world through his words, and to trust that his life had reason and worth beyond that which is measured in moments. All of the pieces in this chapter, and in this book, come together to create the mosaic of Mattie J.T. Stepanek—a child, a young man, a person, a being, who was determined to remind us all that he represents just one small gift in the collective mosaic of humanity, and life.

Camp Tears

Tears of happiness from above,
Tears of sadness from below,
Tears of Heaven for those I love,
Tears of eyes, from my heart, my soul.
I've heard one thousand bells each ring,
Yet, not one of them is mine,
How I long and ache for my Angel Wings,
The gift of eternal Heaven-Time.
Tears of happiness from above,
Tears of sadness from below,
Tears of earth from those I Love,
Tears of eyes, remember my heart, my soul.

June 22, 2003

187

Dear Racheal

Racheal found the footholds,
The handholds in each tree.
Racheal climbed the laddered-stair,
Not grasped by you, or me.
I've seen the path
To Heaven's hold,
My fingers touched the wood,
But dear Racheal is
The one who passed . . .
How I wish I understood.
She held my hand,
She touched my heart,
Put feathers on my hat.
We sang a song,
We danced a while,
She made me feel "all that."
And though the Crow
Says it's about
Just wanting what you've got,
I say it's still
Just wanting life . . .
When those we love have not.
Racheal found the footholds,
The handholds in each tree.
Racheal climbed the laddered-stair,
Not grasped by you, or me.
I've seen the path
To Heaven's hold,
My fingers touched the wood,
But dear Racheal is
The one who passed . . .
How I wish I understood.

Now knotholes in
My stomach form
When I see trees of such,
Remembering our
Spirit talks
Of Heaven's early touch.
I know she's seen
The face of God,
I know she's beyond pain,
But my soul aches
With "why's" of dying . . .
And a sacred shell, again.

Racheal found the footholds,
The handholds in each tree.
Racheal climbed the laddered-stair,
Not grasped by you, or me.
I've seen the path
To Heaven's hold,
My fingers touched the wood,
But dear Racheal is
The one who passed . . .
How I wish I understood.

Dear Racheal's gone
And life goes on
Despite that empty space,
That empty space
Camped in my heart . . .
'Til I reach Heaven's grace.

Racheal found the footholds,
The handholds in each tree.
Racheal climbed the laddered-stair,
Not grasped by you, or me.
I've seen the path
To Heaven's hold,
My fingers touched the wood,
But dear Racheal is
The one who passed . . .
How I wish I understood.
Dear Racheal is
The one who passed . . .
How I wish I understood.

June 22, 2003

Coming of Age

One day,
Yet all too soon,
My memory will
Simply be a
Silhouette in time.
One day,
Now all too near,
My mortality will
Fade and be
Ashes scattered
In the winds of existence.
One day,
For all to know,
My legacy will
Prayerfully be an
Echo of hope, a
Spiritual home, a
Pinch of peace
For the yearning soul.
One day,
Still too soon and too near
Though it's such that I know,
My eternity will
Forever and for all be
The shape of the life
Which I leave behind.

July 17, 2003

Lovely Lady

I know I'm in love
When the thought of her face
Sends me flying with feelings
And a smile I can't hide.
I know I'm in love
When the sound of her name
Makes my heart race a little
Or a lot with young pride.
I know I'm in love
When her voice in my ear
Sends me flying o'er oceans
From mere words on the phone.
I know I'm in love
When my life seems just fine
As I accept the soft touch
Of her hand in my own.

August 9, 2003

190

Blessing Lesson

Blessings ground us
When our dreams
Dawn with our destiny.
Blessings guide us
When our destiny
Dances with our desires.
Blessings grace us
When our desires
Duplicate our devotion.
Let us pray, then,
That our blessings grow
Into echoes that energize
Our earthly lives,
Daring us to be grounded
In our dreams,
In our destiny,
In our desires,
Granting us and
Guiding us as we
Grow in our devotion
Of what really matters
For living,
For love, and
For Life.

August 17, 2003

Thoughts

I feel the near-distance
Of Life in my life.
And though it feels sad
And lonely and large,
Even the silence of God
Gives me strength,
Turning courage into wisdom,
And wisdom into accepted
Knowledge and understanding . . .
For I live so I'll Live in
The faith of existence.

October 1, 2003

191

Dying for Wings

I still miss and love my friend,
Racheal very much.
She died and went to Heaven
This past summer.
I wonder if she dyes
Her and her sister Rebecca's
Angel Wings to match
Her clothes or mood in Heaven.
Like one day,
Her wings would be black,
And another day,
They would be red,
And then blue.
Knowing my fun and free friend,
She probably is,
And knowing her,
She probably also has a
Rack of wing and hair-dying
Material waiting for me,
So that she may make my wings
All the colors of the world,
Like a giant
Heaven and Earth Rainbow.
And we can all fly together
And make Angels laugh
And living-earth people smile,
And see what happiness
Colors can bring.

October 2, 2003

Message

If I had a mutant power,
I would have Angel Wings,
So that I may fly like the Heavens.
And I would have a healing factor,
So that I would never
Have to worry about pain.
I would also want to make fire,
To light the way.
And I would finally want
Telepathy and telekinesis,
So that I could help
Myself and others by
Merely using a strong mind.
And my mutant name
Would be "Messenger"
Because like all Angels,
I have a great message
That I want to share . . .
World Peace.

October 4, 2003

About Prayer

When I go to my God
On bended knee or any pose,
When I beg for assistance
With my friends or any foes,
When I gush words of joy
Or thoughts of any little thing,
When I go to my God
With whatever prayer I bring . . .

*I've got one foot planted
In my here, now, today,
And one foot planted
In some heartbeat away,
I straddle the line
Of my earth-life and Then,
I touch what I'm creating—
My reality some When.*

When I go to my God
I am revealing my soul,
When I pray for the world
Or my future, every goal,
When I rush thoughts of love
Or faith in any little thing,
When I go to our God
With whatever prayer I bring . . .

*I've got one foot planted
In my here, now, today,
And one foot planted
In some heartbeat away,
I straddle the line
Of my earth-life and Then,
I touch what I'm creating—
My reality some-When.*

*See, prayer is the link between
Our here now and our Then,
Yes, prayer is the connection
Between what will be and what's been.
And, prayer is the answer to
Each prayer within each heart,
Prayer can reassure us
That We're never far apart.*

So I go to my God
On bended knee or any pose,
And I beg for assistance
With my friends or any foes,
Then I gush words of joy
Or faith in any little thing,
And I know that our God
Will hear whatever prayer I bring

*Cause I've got one foot planted
In my here, now, today,
And one foot planted
In some heartbeat away,
I straddle the line
Of my earth-life and Then,
I touch what I'm creating—
My reality some-When.*

November 9, 2003

193

Psalm of Life

Echo of understanding,
Silhouette of courage,
Reflection of knowledge,
Oh, sighing breath of wisdom,
        Spirit my life.

I live in the shadow of doubt,
I dwell in dark of unknown,
I wonder and wander in
Mere mortal moments,
My soul seeking solace and peace.

Echo of understanding,
Silhouette of courage,
Reflection of knowledge,
Oh, sighing breath of wisdom,
        Spirit my life.

I pray for the world in such need,
I yearn for a world with real peace,
I praise and give thanks in
The hope of tomorrows,
Beyond days of my moments on earth.

Echo of understanding,
Silhouette of courage,
Reflection of knowledge,
Oh, sighing breath of wisdom,
        Spirit my life.

November 23, 2003

Thanksgiving Prayer for Sandy

Oh, Great Creator,
We give thanks for friends, and
We give thanks for life, and
We give thanks for unity, and
Harmony and peace and hope.
Oh, Great Creator,
We give thanks
For lessons of the past and
For gifts of the present and
For opportunities of the future.
Oh, Great Creator,
We give thanks for this moment,
As we gather together
To give thanks for this,
The Eternal Feast.
Amen.

November 27, 2003

194

'Tis the Season

The season brings a reason for
Solemn contemplation,
The season brings a reason for
Joyful celebration,
The season brings a reason for
Gentle realization,
That the season brings a reason for
Peace in every nation

> *Let this season be the season*
> *That lasts throughout the year,*
> *Let our reason be the reason*
> *That unites us beyond fear,*
> *Let us join our hearts together*
> *With those far and with those near,*
> *Let us live this gentle moment*
> *In each moment, not just here.*

The reason for the season is
A miracle in life,
The reason for the season then
Can bring an end to strife,
The season and the reason are
The answer to each prayer,
In all seasons, for all reasons,
We must touch our world with care.

> *Let this season be the season*
> *That lasts throughout the year,*
> *Let our reason be the reason*
> *That unites us beyond fear,*
> *Let us join our hearts together*
> *With those far and with those near,*
> *Let us live this gentle moment*
> *In each moment, not just here.*

December 22, 2003

195

Dickens of a Season

Perhaps God will
Send me a dead friend
And three timely ghosts
For Christmas
This year,
Since my soul
Struggles so
With the spirit
Of my season
In this, my brief
Moment of life
Before Life.

December 24, 2003

Spiral Direction

Indeed,
The world does
Not stop spinning
Because I am in pain or
Because tragedy exists . . .
Perhaps,
The world actually
Spins even faster
With the winds of despair . . .
Thus,
The world offers
Chances for
We, the people
On board to
Not fade into breezes of
Missed opportunity,
In deed.

January 1, 2004

Observed

I am
Living
On the edge
Of breath,
Where a
Single
Element
Of a moment
In time
Can make
The difference,
Determining
From which side
Of the veil
Life is viewed
For the
Realization
Of that which
I am.

January 22, 2004

196

Final Heartsongs

About Matters

What really matters
Is choosing
What really matters,
Not merely
Being aware or
Knowing about or
Considering attentively.
What really matters
Is choosing
What really matters
With a clear and
Gentle heart
In all matters.

January 21, 2004

The Ultimate To-Do List

So much to do on earth.
So much more to do in Heaven.
In Heaven, as it is on earth,
It will be children and people first,
For always and for-Ever, then
Mission and fantasy for Ever-after.
My siblings will get big hugs.
Jamie, and Katie and Stevie, and
All the other passed children and I
Will sing and dance and cheer,
"Alleluia, alleluia, amen, alleluia,"
Together, again and finally.
Aunt Margaret and I will meet
And play cards and board games
For as long as she would like, and
Granddaddy Ray can tell me stories
About fishing and Florida, and
The Patron Saints will teach me
The Way of interceding for others.
And God . . .
God will reveal
The reality of Eternity to me
However my Creator chooses
To reveal such wisdom of glory.

After I enjoy a mortal moment
Of my Heavenly fantasies with the
Fellowship, Wizards, and Ewoks in
The Shire, Hogwarts, and Village,
I will be ready for my
Eternal Heavenly duties.
I will paint rainbows, and
I will plant peace, and
I will pinch hope into hearts
For the matter of Forever.
So much to do on earth.
So much more to do in Heaven.
But in Heaven, not as it is on earth,
I will Finally have
"All the time in the world"
To Eternally Live
My ultimate To-Do List,
Singing and dancing and cheering,
"Alleluia, alleluia, amen, alleluia!"

January 25, 2004

Mattie's Dream

And then, I died.
God said to me,
"My child, you are
Blessed with a choice.
You can choose
Five years contemplating
Sins in purgatory, or
You can choose
Fifty years more
Suffering on earth."
Is five years enough?
Five years to think.
An eternity of suffering.
Fifty years to sin.
Didn't the Lord say
That we all do suffer?
I looked up and said,
"My God, You are
Blessing me with choice.
You gave me the gift
Of life and of choice.
What would you
Ask of me, my God?"
And God reached out
To my life and my soul
And hugged me.

February 1, 2004

DJ's Son

Tom has been sick,
And now he's in need
Of re-juveni-hellation.
He will laugh at
Such a thought,
Because he understands
And even appreciates
Concepts like
Spritzophrenic rain,
Which makes it
Difficult to play
After the storm
That never quite ends,
And when I tell him
That my outlook
On my mortal moments
Is rather pissimystic.

February 20, 2004

Vision

I believe
Seashells and
Moons are
Our Lady's
Favorite items.
She is pictured
So often
In their midst.

I believe
She believes
In the sacred
Reminders
Of temples
Though empty
And reflections
Of Light.

February 9, 2004

199

Verge

My mind works
Overtime
All the time
In wake and in sleep
So and too many wakes
For youth
Even one which
So bravely and too boldly
Bears the doom marks
And carries the burdens
And so many joys
That it weighs
So and too heavily . . .
  I cannot hide
From the thoughts
The visions
The daymares
The nightdreads . . .

Every neural portal
And there are many
Is saturated
Brimming with
Another idea
Another memory
Another list
Another what-if
Another when and
Where and
Who and
How but never
An if and never
A why
  For it is
So and too late
So and too often and
So and too much for
Consideration . . .

February 25, 2004

Final Heartsongs

Purple Moon

Sometimes,
I think the world
Would be lovelier
If the moon
Glowed purple
During the darkness . . .
A gentle glimmering ray
Of healing and hope,
Illuminating the earth
And the people . . .
The slow pace
And contemplation
Of lava lamp nights,
Peacefully demonstrating
A quieter,
Gentler way
Of passing time . . .

Oh, reflect upon a
Purple moon, a
Peaceful tune, a
Patient light,
Pacific rune . . .
But sometimes,
When life
Gets in the way,
Blocking the passage
Of night into day,
And I realize the pull
Of the ebbing tide
Is not so far away,
For it is coming,
Ever and too soon,
I don't even know
If it matters for now
If there is purple, or
If there is a moon.

February 29, 2004

Untitled

My mother . . .
To whom railroads are poetic,
Exciting, reminiscent of
Something that might have been,
But one can never be sure of
That something beyond
Somewhere.
Moved by the presence of
Each railroad track,
She captures the pictured
Reality or thought,
And so, too, the sun
In rising or setting,
In full and vivid glory or
In gentle subtle shades of
What was,
What is,
What might be
On the horizon.
My mother . . .
Determined seeker of shortcuts
Regardless of how long it takes
To find such or
To journey much or
To travel to the destination
By these unplanned paths
That twist and wind and
Take you to the side or back
Before going forward.
But always, she says,
See that?
We would have missed that
If we hadn't found this
Shortcut.

And I sigh,
In frustration or
In realization or
Perhaps
In resignation, or
Even celebration
That my mother
Will soon be looking for
Another shortcut
No matter how long it takes.
My mother . . .
Who prays
To the "Cowgods"
To "take her away,"
Or blames it
On the groundhog
During times of stress,
Or sometimes distress
As she ponders.
For direction
Or at least some sign.
A sign of what,
She does not know,
But still,
A sign of something,
Which is better than
Not having a clue,

Even if there is none
To be had.
My mother . . .
Oh, my dear mother,
My friend,
My spirit,
My breath,
My hope,
My teacher,
My laughter,
My snuggles,
My inspiration,
My Heartsong,
My Gracenote,
My more and my
Every and all of life,
"I'll love her forever,
I'll like her for always."
And may she remember
"As long as she's living
Her baby I'll be,"
And may she be comforted,
"For as long as there's Heaven,
Together we'll be . . ."
My mother.

March 5, 2004

203

Teen Meeting Time Capsule

First, this is a Teen Capsule . . .
So ten, fifteen,
However many years later,
You will remember that
This is Mattie,
Reminding the Martin Cabin girls
To turn off your wheelchairs
When you're not moving
To save energy and the battery.
And now, this is a Time Capsule . . .
So however many years later,
You will remember that
I like to read.
To Kill a Mockingbird.
The Giver. Moby Dick.
I do some serious reading.
To Kill a Mockingbird
Is also my favorite movie, but
It has to be in Black and White.
You know, being in color
Takes away the message.
The Lord of the Rings:
Return of the King, which won
Eleven Oscars in the year 2004,
Rocks as my second favorite movie.
I like video games,
Going out shopping,
Going to the theater,
And you know, I also like to eat.
Me and my stomach.
I actually love vegetables.
I like them raw better than cooked.
Carrots, broccoli, peas, celery,
You name it, I'll eat it.
But for every veggie I consume,
I can also eat a piece of junk food.

In real food, I like barbeque ribs,
And I love crabs.
At summer camp, they have
To reserve a whole batch for me.
I'll clean out the entire ocean!
You will remember that
I like having friends.
I like hanging out with people,
My family, anyone who helps me,
My camp counselor, Devin, whose
Blond hair streaked gray after
All these years with me.
I also love my mom,
She's the biggest part of my life,
And my service dog, Micah.
And finally,
This is my Time Capsule . . .
So as in all years, I will get a
Little deeper for remembering, that
MDA Summer Camp is the
Highlight, the holiday, of my year.
Even more for remembering, is that
I like being able to wake up each day,
Be able to say, "I'm alive!" and
Know I'm saying and processing it.
I like just being able to see
The sunrise, and sunset, every day
In one piece, and have the breath
To say "thank You" for such gifts.
Here, I will stop leaving memories
For this Time Capsule,
So ten, fifteen,
However many years later,
You may remember these things
That mattered to a teen named Mattie.

March 6, 2004

Final Heartsongs

Final Thoughts

Have you ever wondered
If some people will cry, and cry
And sigh after you die?
Have you wondered
If the people will cry and then
Try to move forward as time
Fades the wounds and
Dries the tears and
Gracefully blesses the soul?
I have.
I have so
Wondered.
Have you ever wondered
If some people will live, and live
And love differently after you pass?
Have you wondered
If the people will live and then
Sift and reflect on the
Wisdom of your thoughts and the
Gentleness of your words and the
Enduring consequences of your actions?
I have.
I have so, so
Wondered.
Have you ever wondered
If some people will wonder, and wonder
And wander in realization after reality rests?
Have you wondered
If the people will wonder and then
Peacefully ponder the undying
Essence of your echo and the
Silhouette of your legacy that
Spirits the memory after death passes?
I have.
I have so, so, so
Wondered.

March 7, 2004

205

Final Words

I am a man
Of many thoughts
And,
I am a man
Of many, many words.

May 10, 2004

Have I done enough?
Will it last?

May 22, 2004

Amen.
I love you.

June 21, 2004

Yes.

June 22, 2004

206

Epilogue

I will revolve seasonally
When my death comes,
And children will remember
And share their Heartsongs,
Celebrating the gifts in the circle of life.

Excerpt from "Eternal Role Call" by Mattie J.T. Stepanek,
in *Celebrate Through Heartsongs* (Hyperion/VSP, 2002)

PREVIOUS PAGE: Firefighters lower Mattie's casket from a fire truck before his funeral, June 2004

TOP: Mattie and his mom celebrating a sunset in Nags Head, North Carolina, summer 1993

BOTTOM LEFT: Mattie enjoying a sunset in Nags Head, North Carolina, summer 2000

BOTTOM RIGHT: Mattie touching life gently, summer 1998

"Ode To Mattie"
(by Jerry Lewis)

Mattie is gone . . .
And so is my spirit
A piece of my heart feels gone as well . . .
How do we fill that void?
How do we tell our emotional
System it will recover . . .
Maybe it will, but it will never be the same . . .
How do we go on without Mattie's presence?
We have to . . .
And we'll probably be all right if we carry what Mattie was
And what he believed the world was all about,
If we follow his understanding about life and love
We can't go wrong . . . (And the child shall lead us)
Good-bye Mattie, my friend, and young champion . . .
I will miss you very much . . .
And this Labor Day will be your day, Mattie,
And I will keep you in the forefront of my mind to get
The money to help so many other kids just like you.
I love you my friend,
I'll be seeing you . . .

Jerry's line, "A piece of my heart feels gone as well" . . . made me think of Mattie's poem "First Anniversary Prayer" from his book Loving Through Heartsongs *(Hyperion/VSP, 2003). A part of that poem reads:* My Heartsong felt so sad that/ It crumbled into little pieces./ And Now, I am so Sad./ But even though my heart is broken,/ I still have all the pieces inside, and/ I can put them back together again. *You know, as I think about those words that Mattie wrote, I smile and I shake my head because he left us a blueprint. He left us a detailed map, step-by-step instructions, to not only mend our broken Heartsongs, but to make the world a better and more peaceful place in the process.*

Epilogue

Mattie called memories "a great gift." I think some of the shattered pieces of my heart will come back together when I let my memories of Mattie flow freely. That sparkle in his eye. That innocent, yet mischievous grin. Simply the way he would push his glasses back to the bridge of his nose. Memories of the long and loving looks, often across very crowded rooms, between Jeni and Mattie, and Mattie and Jeni.

My forever memory, that Mattie became my daughter's first crush and how they created quite a scene when a security guard fussed at them in the parking lot during the middle of the Telethon broadcast. With Katherine in his lap and Mattie breaking all ground speed records, the guard was sure they would get run over. Jeni, with her ever-watchful eye, assured me they hadn't been in any real danger. In fact, it was the Telethon cars and limos and shuttle buses in danger of those two running over them.

I think, in addition to memories, another part of Mattie's heart-healing blueprint is of course playing. Could he not turn us almost instantly into wonderful, playful children? Laughing, celebrating life, being downright irreverent at times—Can I say "fart machine" today [here in a church]? And from that playful child state, he put us in a frame of mind that brought back a touch of innocence in all of us. And from that innocence, hope. And from hope, the elusive peace.

I will keep putting the pieces of my heart together by following Mattie's call to action. When Mattie's poems are read, those actions are quite clear: Share kind thoughts, words, and deeds; always forgive; let us think gently, speak gently, live gently; be patient with yourself and others; be good everywhere you are and go; practice flowing thoughtfulness; never give up in things that matter; and, always and always and always believe in the Light and the angels . . .

I had never met anyone that I thought had possibly lived on this earth before. But that's what I felt when I met Mattie. I had never met anyone before that I thought God had given back to Earth. But that's what I felt when I met Mattie. I had never met anyone before that I thought was a real angel. I don't think I even really believed in earthbound angels. But then I met Mattie. After leaving this huge imprint on us, how do we now repair our crumbled hearts? Recall his memories often, play, and then play some more, practice peace. With the tools that Mattie himself gave each and every one of us, our Heartsongs will be whole again. Thank you Mattie. We love you.

—Jann Carl
(Host of the weekend version of *Entertainment Tonight*)

Excerpts from Tribute by Jann Carl during the funeral of Mattie J.T. Stepanek on June 28, 2004, Wheaton, Maryland

Epilogue

Eyes

by Mattie J.T. Stepanek
December 8, 2003

Chapter 2

June, never mind the year.

> "A reading from the book of Revelation:
> "I, John, your brother who share with you . . ."

Stephen looked around and was pleased. In his mind, he listened to Father Larette, who died when Stephen was only seven years old. Father Larette's voice was commanding, yet not demanding. Listening to him read from the Holy Bible lifted Stephen up with a gentle, wise breeze of heavenly wind and sent him flying into the deepest parts of his spirit where he could be one with himself and God, meditating on the meaning of every Scripture, the Lesson of every parable, and the beauties of all things created, from the winter's warm sun reflecting upon the harsh coldness of the mortal Earth to the smallest blade of summer's soft grass. There were no illusions for Stephen. He wanted the truth. He had the truth.

Outside, the seasons would come and go as they would in any other life. Many of his acquaintances chose to alter time. It was an eternal summer with a light breeze, or autumn trees never ceasing to drop their orange rainbows. Others chose to have a holiday every day, or to never leave their bed, or to always be moving. But not for Stephen. For Stephen, seasons would come and go normally as they would in Stephen's life, and, in his eyes, as they should. Christmas would come once a year, as well as every other holiday. Rain would fall, as would leaves, snow, or the sun's golden rays. There would be days that would be miserably cold, or unbearably hot, or dull, wet, and gray. Not every winter had snow. Not every summer was perfect. Stephen wanted it that way, for he appreciated God's truth that He enclosed in the Creation of everything. Stephen believed that each day, each moment, had reason, meaning, and some beauty or lesson to behold, or else God would not have created it. Even a day in which the weather was horrible and nothing went as planned or as hoped had beauty and meaning in Stephen's eyes.

The doors of the Church were always wide open, as were the arms of Father Larette, who Stephen considered the greatest Holy influence in his life apart from God himself. In his life,

Stephen wished that he could always be at Church, where he could meditate, pray, think and reflect, and be at peace. But Stephen and his family only went twice a week. That was not how Stephen wanted it. He placed God before all things in his life, even his mortal soul. He was proud of his devotion to his Creator, but humbled himself. In Stephen's view, that was the way everyone should act, that people should thank God for having the gifts of life, color, free will, and all that God gave to humanity when shaping humanity in His image. Stephen thanked God for all, and tried his best to never stray from God's face by sinning against Him. Steven never bore false witness about his love and devotion for God. Stephen always smiled upon his enemies and up to Heaven. He turned the other cheek no matter how much it angered or hurt or saddened him to do so. And, even in the end, when a dark death awaited him if he did not "answer correctly," he was always honest about what he believed in.

"This is the Word of the Lord," finished Larette, as he kneeled to the Bible and put it back in its stand, and then gave a smile to Stephen, as he always did after the reading when he was alive on Earth.

"Thanks be to God," answered Stephen along with all of the other Seraphim and Cherubim at Stephen's Mass, who, as well, were Angels who chose to come listen to Father Larette's voice, not illusions. Stephen smiled and thanked God once more in this heart. This was Stephen's Heaven.

Index of Titles

And all of the pages
Would have lots and lots of words, filled with
Mattie's thoughts and Heartsongs.
And they would live and teach
Saying "Hooray for Life" forever,
Even after I am gone.

Excerpt from "The Mattie Book" by Mattie J.T. Stepanek,
in *Journey Through Heartsongs* (Hyperion/VSP, 2002)

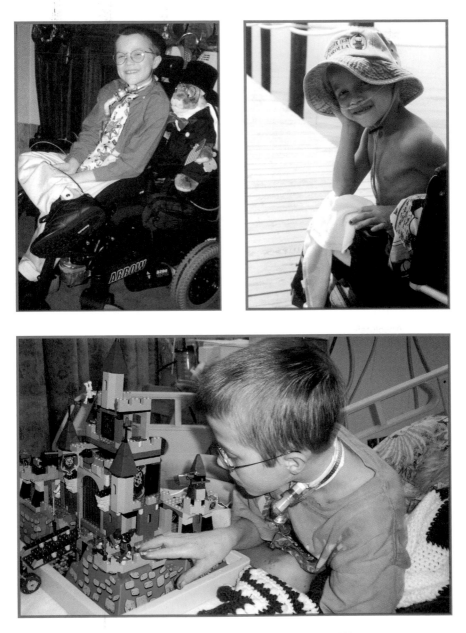

PREVIOUS PAGE: Mattie in his wizard hat during a book signing, December 2001

TOP LEFT: Mattie getting ready for a speech, fall 2002

TOP RIGHT: Mattie in his classic fishing hat, summer 1999

BOTTOM: Mattie playing with Legos during a stay in the Pediatric ICU, spring 2003

Index of Titles

Index of Titles

Index of Titles

Reflections of a Peacemaker

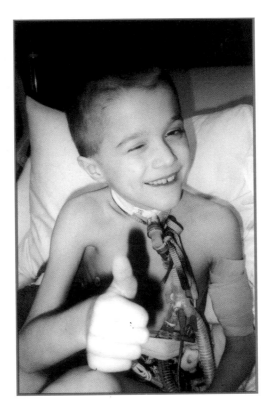

In this *Portrait Through Heartsongs* we realize
the mosaic of Mattie J.T. Stepanek—"a poet, a
peacemaker, and a philosopher who played."
In the closing essay of this book, "Eyes," we are
given a glimpse of what Mattie believed was
the reward for a good life—Heaven, which, in
his eyes, was the fullness of life all over again.
In accepting the commission to carry Mattie's
message further, each reader is now chal-
lenged to go forth and, looking in the mirror,
seek the *Reflections of a Peacemaker*.